CITYPACK TOP 25
Vancouver

TIM JEPSON

If you have any comments
or suggestions for this guide
you can contact the editor at
Citypack@theAA.com

AA Publishing
Find out more about AA Publishing and the wide
range of services the AA provides by visiting our
website at www.theAA.com/bookshop

How to Use This Book

KEY TO SYMBOLS

✚ Map reference to the accompanying fold-out map

✉ Address

☎ Telephone number

🕐 Opening/closing times

🍴 Restaurant or café

🚆 Nearest rail station

🚊 Nearest light-rail station

🚌 Nearest bus route

⛴ Nearest ferry route/stop

♿ Facilities for visitors with disabilities

❓ Other practical information

▷ Further information

ℹ Tourist information

✋ Admission charges: Expensive (over $20), Moderate ($10–$20), and Inexpensive (under $10)

★ Major Sight ★ Minor Sight

👣 Walks 🚍 Excursions

🎁 Shops

🎵 Entertainment and Nightlife

🍽 Restaurants

This guide is divided into four sections

• Essential Vancouver: An introduction to the city and tips on making the most of your stay.
• Vancouver by Area: We've broken the city into five areas, and recommended the best sights, shops, entertainment venues, nightlife and restaurants in each one. Suggested walks help you to explore on foot.
• Where to Stay: The best hotels, whether you're looking for luxury, budget or something in between.
• Need to Know: The info you need to make your trip run smoothly, including getting about by public transport, weather tips, emergency phone numbers and useful websites.

Navigation In the Vancouver by Area chapter, we've given each area its own color, which is also used on the locator maps throughout the book and the map on the inside front cover.

Maps The fold-out map accompanying this book is a comprehensive street plan of Vancouver. The grid on this fold-out map is the same as the grid on the locator maps within the book. We've given grid references within the book for each sight and listing.

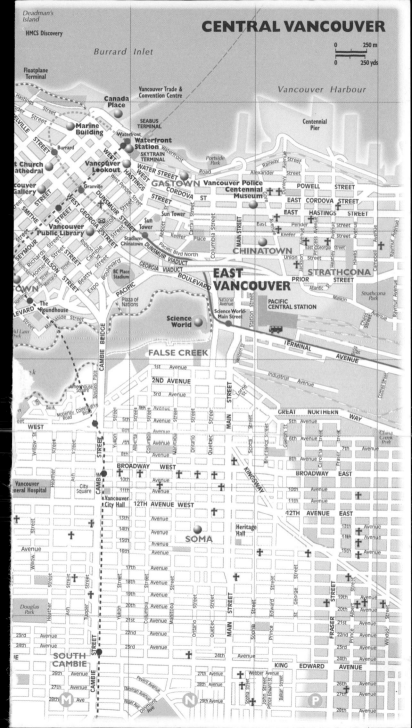

Contents

CONTENTS

Introducing Vancouver

Vancouver is a beautiful city, fringed by the ocean and framed by majestic mountains. A relaxed city, rich in the pleasures of the outdoors, it is also a place blessed with fine museums, superb parks, cafés and some of North America's best restaurants.

No wonder, then, that it is often voted the world's best city in which to live. Few other cities—not Sydney, not Rio, not San Francisco—have a setting as sublime, or an appeal that combines a clean, safe urban environment; North America's largest city park; magnificent hiking trails; year-round skiing; sailing, kayaking and whale-watching in pristine waters; a world-class orchestra and leading opera, theater and dance companies; cutting-edge contemporary arts; and a welcoming and integrated multicultural population. And all this in a city that—in its present guise—is barely 150 years old.

Vancouver is also a city with zest and dynamism, booming economically, bolstered by its ever-increasing trade with Asia—the port is one of the world's busiest—and flushed with pride at having been awarded the 2010 Winter Olympic Games. It is also a thriving center for film and TV production—third in North America behind Los Angeles and New York—and a place where shopping and nightlife, whether a funky bar or classical concert, and artistic and cultural life, are the equal of almost any city in the world.

True, the weather outside the sunny summer months can be dismal, and parts of east Vancouver have a gritty edge at odds with the cosmopolitan élan of the sleek Downtown core, but it's hard to see anyone being disappointed with a city whose inhabitants, surveys reveal, read more, drink more wine, smoke less, spend more on outdoor equipment, and support more bars and restaurants than anywhere else in Canada. And even if Vancouver does pale, then there is always Victoria, British Columbia's charming and easily visited provincial capital, just across the water on Vancouver Island.

Facts + Figures

- Population: 578,041 (Greater Vancouver: 2,116,581) in 2006
- Canada's third-largest city
- Size: 114.67sq km (44.26sq miles)
- Tourism: $3.1 billion annually
- 8 million overnight visitors annually

WINTER OLYMPICS

July 2 2003 was a big day for Vancouver: Official word reached thousands of city citizens and officials from Prague that Vancouver had been awarded the 2010 Winter Olympic and Paralympic Games, beating off bids from Pyeongchang in South Korea and Salzburg in Austria.

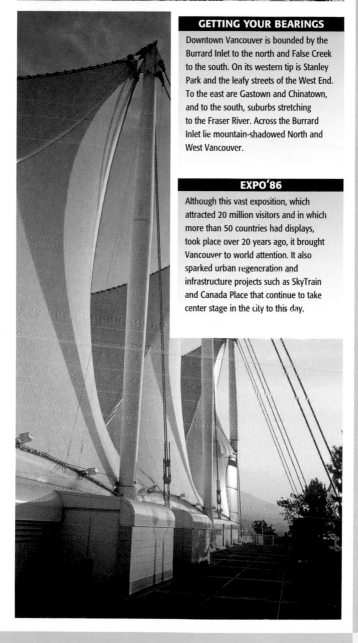

GETTING YOUR BEARINGS

Downtown Vancouver is bounded by the Burrard Inlet to the north and False Creek to the south. On its western tip is Stanley Park and the leafy streets of the West End. To the east are Gastown and Chinatown, and to the south, suburbs stretching to the Fraser River. Across the Burrard Inlet lie mountain-shadowed North and West Vancouver.

EXPO'86

Although this vast exposition, which attracted 20 million visitors and in which more than 50 countries had displays, took place over 20 years ago, it brought Vancouver to world attention. It also sparked urban regeneration and infrastructure projects such as SkyTrain and Canada Place that continue to take center stage in the city to this day.

A Short Stay in Vancouver

DAY 1

Morning Visit **Canada Place** (▷ 24–25) for the perfect introduction to the city and wonderful views of the port and mountains, plus a promenade that offers an insight into Vancouver's history.

Mid-morning Walk east to **Gastown** (▷ 46–47), perhaps visiting the **Vancouver Lookout** (▷ 49) en route. **Chinatown** (▷ 44–45), and the Dr. Sun Yat-Sen Garden in particular, is an optional extension if you hurry.

Lunch Have dim sum in one of Chinatown's many restaurants or return to Gastown and the **Water Street Café** (▷ 60). Or take a bus or taxi back to **Downtown** for one of its many dining options (▷ 38–40).

Afternoon Follow the **Coal Harbour Seawalk** (▷ 32) west of Canada Place along the waterfront to **Stanley Park** (▷ 26–27).

Mid-afternoon Explore Stanley Park, either on foot, or by renting a bike. Perhaps visit the **Vancouver Aquarium** (▷ 28) then walk down Denman Street to **English Bay** (▷ 32). Take a bus or taxi or walk back to central Downtown, perhaps via **Barclay Square** (▷ 30).

Dinner Downtown is crammed with restaurants: **Earls** (▷ 38–39) and the more expensive **CinCin** (▷ 38) are two excellent and relaxed options. The **White Spot** (▷ panel, 39) chain is perfect for families.

Evening Stroll up and down Robson Street, Downtown's main thoroughfare, where the shops stay open late and which buzzes with activity on summer nights.

DAY 2

Morning Aim for an early start and take the **SeaBus** (▷ 87) to North Vancouver. At **Lonsdale Quay** (▷ 88), take a bus or taxi to **Grouse Mountain** (▷ 84).

Mid-morning After an hour or so up the mountain, walk or take a bus to see the sights of the **Capilano River** (▷ 82–83), notably the Salmon Hatchery and, perhaps, the popular Capilano Suspension Bridge.

Lunch Return by taxi or bus to Lonsdale Quay and buy a picnic, snack or take-out meal from the market and its many cafés and food stalls. Sit on the boardwalk and admire the view of Vancouver's Downtown skyline across the water.

Afternoon Return to Downtown by SeaBus and walk or take a taxi to **Yaletown** (▷ 50–51), spending an hour exploring before taking a ferry to Granville Island. Alternatively, take a bus or taxi from Downtown to the **Museum of Anthropology** (▷ 67).

Mid-afternoon You'll need an hour at least to see **Granville Island** (▷ 65) and its superb market.

Dinner Have a drink or early dinner on Granville Island, perhaps at **Bridges** (▷ 75), **Sandbar** (▷ 78) or the **Backstage Lounge** (▷ 75). Or return to Yaletown and dress up a little for **Cioppino's** (▷ 59) or the **Blue Water Café** (▷ 59).

Evening Yaletown offers bars galore: Try the **Yaletown Brewing Company** (▷ 58) or **Capone's** (▷ 57) for drinks and jazz.

Top 25

►►►

Butchart Gardens
▷ **94–95** These popular gardens are one of the key sights close to Victoria.

Canada Place ▷ **24–25** Visit this striking building for wonderful views of the port and mountains.

Capilano River ▷ **82–83** Beautiful river valley, with trails, suspension bridge and salmon hatchery.

Yaletown ▷ **50–51** Vancouver's trendiest Downtown area is a former warehouse district of bars, shops and restaurants.

Whistler ▷ **101** A winter and summer recreational resort and the main focus of the 2010 Winter Olympics.

Whale-watching ▷ **100** See whales on an excursion from Victoria.

West End ▷ **30** Beaches, leafy streets and funky Denman Street characterize this popular neighborhood.

Victoria ▷ **98–99** A charming small city, and an essential part of any visit.

Vancouver Museum ▷ **69** Explore the city's history at this museum.

Vancouver Maritime Museum ▷ **68** Models, maps and photographs help to evoke Vancouver's maritime heritage.

Vancouver Lookout ▷ **49** Dizzying external elevators take you to a lofty platform for dazzling views.

Vancouver Art Gallery ▷ **29** Renowned for the works of Emily Carr and its contemporary exhibitions.

Vancouver Aquarium ▷ **28** Dolphins and whales are the stars of this leading visitor attraction.

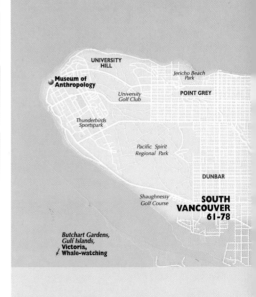

These pages are a quick guide to the Top 25, which are described in more detail later. Here they are listed alphabetically, and the tinted background shows which area they are in.

Chinatown ▷ 44–45
A world apart, full of ethnic markets, bustling streets and a Chinese garden.

Gastown ▷ 46–47
Vancouver's historic heart is a rejuvenated district of shops, bars and restaurants.

Granville Island ▷ 65
A superb market, views and captivating shops and galleries.

Grouse Mountain ▷ 84
Glorious views and activities aplenty, amid wild scenery.

Gulf Islands ▷ 96
Picturesque islands between Vancouver and Vancouver Island.

H.R. MacMillan Space Centre ▷ 66 Revel in the interactive displays and shows here.

Lynn Canyon Park ▷ 85
This pretty forest enclave offers waterfalls, canyons and lots of hiking trails

Mount Seymour Provincial Park ▷ 86
Semi-wilderness in North Vancouver, with many hiking and mountain-biking opportunities.

Museum of Anthropology ▷ 67 Art and artifacts of First Nations peoples and a superb collection of totems.

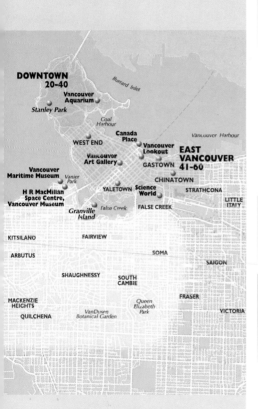

DOWNTOWN
20–40

Burrard Inlet

Vancouver Aquarium

Stanley Park

Coal Harbour

Canada Place

Vancouver Harbour

WEST END

Vancouver Lookout

EAST VANCOUVER
41–60

Vancouver Art Gallery

GASTOWN

Vancouver Maritime Museum

Vanier Park

CHINATOWN

YALETOWN

Science World

STRATHCONA

H R MacMillan Space Centre, Vancouver Museum

False Creek

FALSE CREEK

LITTLE ITALY

Granville Island

KITSILANO

FAIRVIEW

ARBUTUS

SOMA

SAIGON

SHAUGHNESSY

SOUTH CAMBIE

FRASER

MACKENZIE HEIGHTS

Queen Elizabeth Park

VICTORIA

QUILCHENA

VanDusen Botanical Garden

Stanley Park ▷ 26–27
North America's largest city park, with many recreational possibilities.

SeaBus ▷ 87 Ride the ferry to North Vancouver for superb views of the port and city skyline.

Science World ▷ 48
A futuristic building houses a fun science museum full of interactive exhibits.

◄ ◄ ◄

Shopping

Vancouver offers excellent shopping, including all the international chains and designer names you'd expect of any major city, as well as a wide range of markets, galleries, boutiques and specialist stores. It also offers well-defined shopping areas, from the glitz of Downtown and funky streets of Yaletown to the allure of Granville Island and the younger, cutting-edge Main Street and Commercial Drive.

Shopping Downtown

Downtown's main shopping thoroughfare is Robson Street, notably the stretch near the intersection with Burrard Street. In the past, this area was devoted to small stores and European restaurants, but it is now the site of flagship stores such as Banana Republic, Roots, Nike, Zara and other major national and international chains. Downtown also contains many of the city's major malls (▷ 34) and department stores for excellent one-stop shopping for a wide range of goods.

Other Shopping Areas

Gastown, too, has changed, its many souvenir shops gradually giving way to more interesting stores, notably designer clothes and homeware outlets. Yaletown and parts of Kitsilano have a similar profile, mixing upscale galleries with fashion, furniture and home-design shops. Granville Island remains what it always was—a collection of varied craft, design and specialist stores clustered around the superb food market.

MARKETS

Markets of a different kind can be found in Chinatown, notably a vivid summer night market (▷ 55), as well as in other ethnic districts such as the Punjabi Market on Main Street, one of two streets—with Commercial Drive (▷ 56)—in the city's eastern suburbs where the more adventurous shopper will be rewarded with junk shops, vintage clothing stores and an altogether edgier retail experience.

Top to bottom: Fashion in the SoMa District; jewelry at one of the many markets; a cookery bookstore

Specialist Stores
Vancouver offers all the usual fun Canadian staples you might want as a souvenir or gift—maple syrup, say, or a traditional Hudson's Bay Company blanket—but it is also a premier destination for various specialist purchases. Foremost among these is camping and outdoor equipment, with keen prices and a large number of outdoor stores, many of them close to one another in south Vancouver (▷ 74). You'll also find lots of good boarding, cycling and other sports equipment stores. Chinatown has novelties, gastronomic and otherwise, though you'll find superb food everywhere, not least in Granville Island (but check import restrictions before taking foodstuffs home). Vintage clothing stores cluster in Gastown's side streets, along with a large number of stores selling Cuban and other cigars.

Arts and Crafts
Galleries in the city offer some of North America's finest Inuit and other First Nations art and artifacts, notably in Gastown. Some of these deal in works that cost thousands of dollars, but you can also pick up less expensive ethnic items or mementoes in the gallery shop at the Museum of Anthropology (▷ 67), among other places. Vancouver is also full of artists and artisans, and many shopping areas (Granville Island in particular) have commercial galleries and craft workshops.

TAX REFUNDS
Most goods are priced exclusive of a five percent Goods and Services Tax (GST), and, often, a seven percent Provincial Sales Tax (PST). Visitors can reclaim GST on total purchases over $200. Each individual purchase must be over $50. Original receipts must be stamped at designated refund offices or shops at the port of departure and returned, with proof of travel, with a completed rebate form, available in most stores, hotels or visitor centers. Visit www.ccra.gc.ca/visitors for more information.

Top to bottom: An interiors store in Yaletown; treats from a city market; hiking supplies

Shopping by Theme

Whether you're looking for a department store, a gallery of Inuit art or something entirely different, you'll find it in Vancouver. On this page shops are listed by theme. For a more detailed write-up, see the individual listings in Vancouver by Area.

ART AND ANTIQUES

Coastal Peoples Fine Arts Gallery (▷ 55)
Deeler's Antiques (▷ panel, 55)
Equinox Gallery (▷ 73)
Images for a Canadian Heritage (▷ 55)
Inuit Gallery of Vancouver (▷ 55)
Legends (▷ panel, 55)
Shaughnessy Antique Gallery (▷ 74)
Spirit Wrestler Gallery (▷ 56)

ARTISAN

Craftshouse Gallery (▷ panel, 73)
Gallery of BC Ceramics (▷ panel, 73)
Jade (▷ 56)

BOOKS AND MAGAZINES

Barbara-Jo's Books to Cooks (▷ 73)
Chapters (▷ 34)
Kidsbooks (▷ 73)
Magpies (▷ panel, 56)
Mayfair News (▷ 74)

FASHION AND ACCESSORIES

Aritzia (▷ 34)
Atomic Model (▷ 55)
Betsey Johnson (▷ 34)
Club Monaco (▷ 34)
Deluxe Junk (▷ 55)
Gravity Pope (▷ 73)
John Fluevog (▷ 56)
Lululemon (▷ 35)
Mark James (▷ 74)
Mintage Vintage (▷ 56)
Richard Kidd (▷ 56)
Roots (▷ 35)
True Value Vintage (▷ 35)
Virgin Mary's (▷ panel, 56)

FOOD AND WINE

Les Amis du Fromage (▷ 73)
Dutch Girl Chocolates (▷ panel, 56)
Kaplan's (▷ 73)
Meinhardt Fine Foods (▷ 74)
Murchies, Vancouver (▷ 35)
Murchies, Victoria (▷ panel, 105)
Purdy's (▷ 74)
Roger's Chocolates (▷ panel, 105)
T & T Supermarket (▷ 56)
Urban Fare (▷ 56)
The Wine Barrel (▷ panel, 105)

INTERIOR DESIGN

Birks (▷ 34)
Chintz (▷ 55)
The Cross (▷ 55)
Inform Interiors (▷ 55)

MARKETS, MALLS AND DEPARTMENT STORES

The Bay (▷ 34)
Chinatown Night Market (▷ 55)
Granville Island (▷ panel, 73)
Holt Renfrew (▷ 35)
The Landing (▷ 56)
Lonsdale Quay Market (▷ 88)
Pacific Centre (▷ panel, 34)
Sears (▷ 35)
Sinclair Centre (▷ 35)

OUTDOOR AND SPORTS EQUIPMENT

A J Brooks (▷ panel, 74)
Comor Outdoor (▷ 73)
Mountain Equipment Co-op (▷ 74)
Pacific Boarder (▷ panel, 74)
Sigge's (▷ 74)
Valhalla (▷ panel, 74)

SPECIALIST

Casa del Habano (▷ 34)
Eyes on Burrard (▷ 34)
HMV (▷ 35)
Zulu Records (▷ 74)

Vancouver by Night

Vancouver is a cultured and hedonistic city, packed with clubs and bars of every type, and with a rich and diverse schedule of festivals, plays, concerts and recitals.

Performing Arts

The city has a broad-minded, cosmopolitan and multiethnic population, its diversity reflected in the city's vast range of cultural activities. Classical music is widely represented, with the world-class Vancouver Symphony Orchestra well to the fore, as are dance and theater. Countless festivals throughout the year showcase most aspects of the performing arts.

Bars and Clubs

Many bars have decks (terraces), usually with fine views. Neighborhood pubs, plus microbreweries serving their own and other specialist ales, are also popular, along with lounges. At most places you order from a waiter or waitress, rather than at the bar.

Loud and Lively

Vancouver also has plenty of louder dance clubs and venues devoted to live music. Most are in Gastown, Yaletown and Downtown (the big, crowd-pleasing places are mostly on Granville Street), though the edgier, fly-by-night clubs and events are usually around Main Street and Commercial Drive. These streets also play host to gay and lesbian clubs— Vancouver has a thriving gay and lesbian community, especially in parts of the West End.

NEED TO KNOW

Nightclubs usually open at around 9pm (though not much happens for a couple of hours) and close any time after 2 or 3am (perhaps earlier Mon–Thu). Bars and lounges may well also open during the day. The line between bars and restaurants is blurry as bars always serve food. Club admission ranges from about $5–$20, though admission for women is often free before 11pm; some clubs insist on a minimum age of 19 or 25.

Vancouver offers a wealth of entertainment and nightlife to suit all tastes

Eating Out

Food in Vancouver is exceptional, thanks to a combination of superb local ingredients, innovative and pioneering chefs, a population that loves to eat out, and the richness and variety of cuisines bequeathed by the city's multiethnic population.

Among the Best
The range and quality of dining options—by common consent—is on a par with cities such as London, Sydney and New York. Vancouver champions the fusion of Asian, Italian and other cuisines, and insists on seasonal, organic and locally sourced ingredients.

A World of Tastes
The choice is vast, from restaurants that serve the traditional forest and mountain foods of the area's First Nations peoples to the cuisines of Korean, Thai, Japanese, Chinese and other ethnic populations. This said, Italian and French influences are often present, as are classic North American staples and fish and seafood, superlative wild salmon in particular.

Need to Know
On the whole, dining out in this most laid-back of cities is a relaxed and informal affair. This is especially true in summer, when many restaurants open their terraces. Prices are lower than you might pay for the equivalent meal in Europe, and portions, as elsewhere in North America, are often generous.

DINING FOR LESS

Vancouver locals love their cafés and their caffeine—actress Bette Midler, after performing in the city, said she had "never seen so much coffee in all my life." You are never far from an excellent café for snacks or a light meal (often with outdoor seating and a lovely view), but the city also has lots of inexpensive Thai diners, Japanese noodle bars and Chinese places for dim sum. Note, too, that bars and pubs always serve food, usually at lower prices than restaurants.

Both casual and more formal dining experiences offer tempting and diverse choices

Restaurants by Cuisine

There are restaurants to suit all tastes and budgets in Vancouver. On this page they are listed by cuisine. For a more detailed description of each restaurant, see Vancouver by Area.

ASIAN AND INDIAN

Floata Seafood (▷ 59)
Guu (▷ panel, 38)
Hapa Izakaya (▷ panel, 38)
Hon's Wun-Tun House
    (▷ 60)
Imperial (▷ 39)
Kirin Mandarin (▷ 40)
Phnom Penh (▷ 60)
Pink Pearl (▷ 60)
Vij's (▷ 78)

BELGIAN

Chambar (▷ 59)

CAFÉS

Arbutus (▷ 77)
Blethering Place
    (▷ panel, 106)
Demitasse (▷ 105)
Gallery Cafe (▷ 39)
Ingrid's Village Café
    (▷ 106)
Pane from Heaven (▷ 78)
Prospect Point Café (▷ 40)
Rebar (▷ 106)

CHAIN RESTAURANTS

Earls (▷ 38)
Flying Wedge (▷ panel, 39)
Joey's (▷ panel, 39)
Milestones (▷ panel, 39)
Soupspoons (▷ panel, 39)
White Spot (▷ panel, 39)

FISH AND SEAFOOD

Blue Water Café (▷ 59)
Coast (▷ 59)
C Restaurant (▷ 59)
Fish House at Stanley Park
    (▷ 39)
Galley Patio & Grill (▷ 77)
Go Fish (▷ 77)
Rodney's Oyster Bar (▷ 60)
Salmon House on the Hill
    (▷ 90)

FRENCH

Après (▷ 106)
Bearfoot Bistro (▷ 106)
La Berengerie (▷ 105)
Bistrot Bistro (▷ 77)
Brasserie L'école (▷ 105)
Le Crocodile (▷ 38)
Delilah's (▷ 38)
Le Gavroche (▷ 39)
Lumière (▷ 77)

ITALIAN

CinCin (▷ 38)
Cioppino's (▷ 59)
Il Giardino di Umberto
    (▷ 39)
Gusto di Quattro (▷ 90)
House Piccolo (▷ 105)
Incendio (▷ 60)
Pagliacci's (▷ 106)
Rocky Mountain Flatbread
    Co (▷ 78)
Il Terrazzo (▷ 106)
Water Street Café (▷ 60)

MEXICAN

Lolita's (▷ 40)

VEGETARIAN

The Naam (▷ panel, 40)

WEST COAST

Araxi (▷ 106)
Bishop's (▷ 77)
Citta Bistro (▷ 106)
Diva at the Met (▷ 38)
Gastropod (▷ 77)
Glowbal Grill (▷ 59)
John's Place (▷ 105)
Lift Bar & Grill (▷ 40)
Mo:le (▷ 106)
Observatory (▷ 90)
Raincity Grill (▷ 40)
Sandbar (▷ 70)
Seasons in the Park (▷ 70)
Sequoia Grill at the
    Teahouse (▷ 40)
Social at Le Magasin
    (▷ 60)
Sophie's Cosmic Café
    (▷ 70)
Templeton (▷ 40)
Tomahawk (▷ 90)
Treehouse Café (▷ 105)
West (▷ 78)

WINE BAR/PUB

Bin 941 (▷ 38)
Hummingbird Pub (▷ 105)

If You Like...

However you'd like to spend your time in Vancouver, these top suggestions should help you organize your ideal visit. Each sight or listing has a fuller write-up elsewhere in the book.

TAKING TO THE SKY

Join a seaplane ride (▷ 119) from Vancouver or Victoria for magnificent views.
Ascend the Vancouver Lookout (▷ 49) for a dizzying sky ride and sweeping city views from the lofty observation platform.
Ride the cable cars up Grouse Mountain (▷ 84) or in Whistler (▷ 101) for stunning mountain vistas.

Top to bottom: A seaplane landing in Coal Harbour; view of West End; Stanley Park; the Chinatown Night Market

A WALK IN THE CITY

Stroll around Canada Place (▷ 24–25) for an informative introduction to the city.
Follow the Coal Harbour Seawalk (▷ 32) from Canada Place toward Stanley Park for an easy waterfront walk.
Join the locals and walk all or part of the Stanley Park Seawall (▷ 26).

A HIKE IN THE MOUNTAINS

Spend the day on Mount Seymour (▷ 86) using the hiking and biking trails.
Follow the paths across the river and through the trees in Lynn Canyon Park (▷ 85).
Head for the peaks in Whistler (▷ 101), with hikes for all abilities.

BROWSING IN MARKETS

Tickle your taste buds on Granville Island (▷ 65), which has one of North America's greatest food markets.
Join the bustle of the Chinatown Night Market (▷ 55), full of intriguing sights, smells and sounds.
Cross the water to visit the Lonsdale Quay Market (▷ 88) in North Vancouver.

The historic Sylvia Hotel; whale-watching (below)

A ROOM WITH A VIEW

Check in to one of Fairmont's landmark properties, the Hotel Vancouver or Waterfront (▷ 112).
Ask for an upper floor at the historic Sylvia Hotel (▷ 109) overlooking English Bay.
Choose a high-rise apartment or suite hotel on Robson Street, and request a room with a view (▷ 109–112).

TAKING TO THE WATER

Ride the SeaBus (▷ 87) ferry across the Burrard Inlet for great views of the port and city skyline.
Go whale-watching (▷ 100) in Victoria.
Clamber aboard one of the tiny ferries that crisscross False Creek near Granville Island (▷ 118).

SAVING MONEY

Assemble a picnic for lunch at Granville Island (▷ 65) or Lonsdale Quay (▷ 88) markets.
Visit sights such as the Vancouver Art Gallery (▷ 29) and Museum of Anthropology (▷ 67) on evenings when admission is free.
Buy a transit day pass (▷ 118) and use the buses, SkyTrain and SeaBus as sightseeing tours.

Shopping at a Vancouver food market (above left); the impressive view of Downtown Vancouver from across the Burrard Inlet (left)

Robson Street; Vancouver Aquarium (below)

SPECIALIST SHOPPING

Make straight for Robson Street (▷ 34–35) for the best in national and international designer names and chains.
Wander around Yaletown (▷ 50–51), which is full of fashion, food, design and other stores.
Explore the side streets of Gastown (▷ 46–47), an increasingly varied shopping destination.

THE LAP OF LUXURY

Book a table at Bishop's (▷ 77) to sample some of the city's best contemporary cooking.
Join the celebrities by checking into the Sutton Place Hotel (▷ 112).
Settle down to traditional afternoon tea at the Empress Hotel, Victoria (▷ 98).

HAVING FUN WITH THE KIDS

Watch the whale and dolphin shows at the Vancouver Aquarium (▷ 28).
Revel in the many innovative interactive displays at the futuristic Science World (▷ 48).
Nurture curious young minds at the H.R. MacMillan Space Centre (▷ 66).

STAYING UP LATE

Sample local ales at one of Vancouver and Victoria's microbreweries (▷ 58, 75, 90, 104).
Listen to mellow jazz at O'Douls (▷ 36), The Railway Club (▷ 37), Capone's (▷ 57) or the Cellar or Backstage Lounge (▷ 75).
Dance to the music at a classic club such as the Commodore, Roxy or Yale (▷ 36–37).

Science World (above right); drinks by the water (right)

Vancouver by Area

Downtown

Downtown is the heart of Vancouver, a peninsula bounded by water on three sides and home to sleek skyscrapers, leafy residential streets, a majestic park, superb shops and many of the city's sights, hotels and attractions.

1

seawall   Walk

Siwash Rock   Trail

LION'S GATE BRIDGE

Siwash Rock

Merlees Trail

Racoon Trail

Rawlings Trail

Avison Trail

Reservoir   Trail

Ravine Trail

seawall   Walk

Hanson   Trail

Tunnel Trail

Pipeline

STANLEY

North Creek   Trail

Lake Trail

Beaver Lake

Thompson Trail

PARK

Lake   Trail

Third Beach

Tatlow   Walk

Beaver Lake Trail

Wren   Trail

Road

2

Park   Drive

CAUSEWAY

Ferguson Point

Lover's   Trail

Tatlow   Walk

south creek   Trail

Vancouver Aquarium

Stanley Park

Lees   Trail

Cathedral   Trail

Rawlings Trail

Second Beach

Lost   Lagoon   Drive

Lost Lagoon

Devonian Harbour Park

3

Lost   Lagoon   Drive

Bayshore Drive

Park Lane

Chilco   Street

Haro Street

Robson

WEST

Beach   Avenue

Gilford   Street

DENMAN

STREET

Street

English Bay Beach

Bidwell Street

WEST END

Cardero   Street

Nelson   Street

Roedde House

Haro

Barclay

Pendrell   Street

Nicola

Comox

Street

4

English Bay

Inukshuk Sculpture

Davie   Street

Broughton

Burnaby

Jervis

Street

Bute

Thurlow

BEACH

Harwood

Street

Sunset Beach

AVENUE

PACIFIC

Beach   Avenue

STREET

0   400 m

0   400 yds

Vancouver Aquatic Centre

Beach Ave.

5

BURRARD BRIDGE

J   **K**   **L**

Burrard Inlet

Brockton
Point

Park Drive

Brockton
Oval Trail

Hallelujah
Point

Coal Harbour
Seawalk

Deadman's
Island

Coal
Harbour

HMCS Discovery

Floatplane
Terminal

Vancouver Trade &
Convention Centre

GEORGIA   West   West Hastings Street

Canada
Place

Pender   Street

MELVILLE   STREET

STREET   Alberni   Marine
Building

Street   Street   Burrard   Waterfront

Street   Christ Church
Cathedral

Street

Street   Vancouver
Art Gallery   STREET

STREET   Street

BURRARD

Hornby

HOWE

Granville   Street

M   N

Canada Place

HIGHLIGHTS

- "Promenade into History"
- Boardwalk views
- IMAX cinema
- Port Authority Interpretive Centre

TIPS

- The city's main visitor center (▷ 122) is opposite the entrance to Canada Place.
- Come to Canada Place in the evening to admire the sunset.

Majestic Canada Place, jutting out into the bustling port, is one of Vancouver's major landmarks, and forms a wonderfully panoramic introduction to the city.

Perfect outlook Canada Place began life as the Canadian Pavilion for Expo'86, a world trade fair in 1986. Its arrival began a transformation of the Downtown waterfront that continues to this day. The complex includes a convention center, luxury hotel, IMAX cinema and the city's major cruise-ship terminal, but for most visitors the dazzling panorama from its walkways is the main appeal. It is a view that embraces the port, Stanley Park and the mountains of the North Shore across the Burrard Inlet. The walkways are a "Promenade into History," and there are 44 information boards detailing different aspects of the city and its past,

Canada Place, once the venue for Expo'86, is now a popular entertainment complex renowned for its unusual design and impressive views

making this an ideal introduction to Vancouver on your first morning.

City icon It's no accident that Canada Place's Teflon roof looks like sails, for the building, jutting the length of three city blocks into the harbor, was designed to resemble a ship—a deliberate nod to the vital role of Vancouver's port, past and present. Across the water, watch ships come and go, seaplanes and helicopters skimming the water, and the piles of timber, sulphur and other raw materials on the far shore that help make this one of the busiest ports in North America. The harbor began life in 1864, exporting fence pickets to Australia, and today handles 82.7 million tonnes of cargo annually and turns over $50 billion in trade. Be sure to ride the SeaBus to North Vancouver (▷ 87) for more harbor views.

THE BASICS

www.canadaplace.ca
www.portvancouver.com
www.imax.com/vancouver
✚ M4
✉ 999 Canada Place Way
☎ Canada Place 604/647-7390. IMAX cinema 604/682-IMAX
🕐 Walkways always open. Interpretive Centre Mon–Fri 8–5
💵 Walkways free. IMAX cinema expensive
🍴 Food outlets in convention center
🚇 Waterfront
🚌 6, 44, 50
♿ Excellent

25

Stanley Park

HIGHLIGHTS

● Vancouver Aquarium
● Third Beach
● Second Beach swimming pool
● The Seawall
● Brockton Point totems
● Prospect Point

TIP

● Take the Coal Harbour Seawalk to reach the park on foot from central Downtown.

Vancouver's crowning natural glory is a sublime recreational area that embraces woodland, rain forest, beaches, formal gardens and beautiful semi-wilderness.

Pristine jewel Stanley Park is one of the most beautiful city parks in the world, surrounded by water on three sides and with the mountains of the North Shore as a dramatic backdrop. At 404ha (998 acres) it is also one of the world's largest urban parks—20 percent larger than New York's Central Park—and provides space aplenty for its 8 million visitors a year. It began life as home to the local Salish and Musqueam aboriginal peoples, but was saved for posterity in 1888 by Lord Stanley (Canada's Governor-General from 1888 to 1893), at a time when the adjoining West End (▷ 30) was being developed for residential use.

Clockwise from left: Experience the wilderness of Stanley Park; Thunderbird Park has fine displays of original and contemporary totem poles; the beautifully maintained Stanley Park Flower Garden; the park is a haven for nature lovers and those wanting to escape the bustle of the city; one of many sculptures to be found in the park

THE BASICS

www.vancouver.ca/parks

K2

Entrances at West Georgia Street, Robson Street, Stanley Park Drive and elsewhere

604/257-8400

Always open

Prospect Point Café (▷ 40), Sequoia Grill at the Teahouse (▷ 40), Fish House at Stanley Park (▷ 39)

19 to Stanley Park Loop or 240, 241, 246 and other services along West Georgia Street

Very good

Free

Children's Farmyard

604/257-8530

Feb 7–May 15 Sat–Sun 11–4 (Mar 14–22, Apr 10–13 daily 11–4); May 16–Sep 13 daily 11–4; Sep 15–Jan call or see website for special services

Inexpensive

Miniature Railway

604/257-8531

Feb 7–May 15 Sat–Sun 11–4 (Mar 14–22, Apr 10–13 daily 11–4); May 16–Jun 26 daily 11–4; Jun 27–Sep 8 daily 10.30–5; Sep 12–13 11–4; Sep 15–Jan call or see website for special services

Inexpensive

Activities The highlights are many. Locals and visitors alike flock to the Seawall, the park's perimeter road, walkway and bicycle trail (cycles can be rented easily at several outlets on Denman Street). Explore all or part of its 10.5km (6.5 miles; a free shuttle bus also makes the circuit in summer) or wander at random along some of the park's many interior trails.

Attractions Most people visit the Vancouver Aquarium (▷ 28), a major attraction in its own right. Pick up a map at the main city visitor center (▷ 122) and see the totems at Brockton Point, the Rose and Shakespeare gardens, Prospect Point (for fine views) and Second and Third Beaches. Youngsters will love the Children's Farmyard and Miniature Railway and the pool and playground at Second Beach.

Vancouver Aquarium TOP 25

Beluga whales and sea lions are just a few of the many species you can learn about

THE BASICS

www.vanaqua.org

🔗 L2

✉ 845 Avison Way, Stanley Park

☎ 604/659-3474

🕐 Daily 9.30–7 (closes 5 Oct–Apr)

🍴 On-site café

🚌 19, then 10-minute walk

♿ Excellent

💰 Very expensive

HIGHLIGHTS

● Dolphin and beluga whale shows
● Underwater whale-viewing area
● Underground galleries
● Interactive zone

TIPS

● The aquarium gets very busy so arrive early.
● To ensure a good view, find a place close to the dolphin and whale pools well before the scheduled start of the feeding and other demonstrations.

The aquarium is one of North America's largest marine and science centers, and the most-visited tourist attraction in Canada west of Toronto's CN Tower.

Maritime variety Most visitors to the aquarium, at the heart of Stanley Park, come to see the dolphin shows, little different to similar shows in theme parks the world over. However, the complex also contains many thousands of other sea creatures, representing at least 600 different species. Like the Stanley Park Zoo before it (now closed), the aquarium has been criticized by environmentalists, and is now trying to shift its emphasis to research and conservation projects.

Mostly mammals This said, most of the big draws, after the dolphins, are the larger mammals—seals, sharks, walruses, and some playful sea otters—that are confined to only moderate-size pools. The whales have a slightly larger area with vast underwater glass viewing panels. These areas become crowded, but you can book behind-the-scenes tours and sleepovers.

Arctic to Amazon Most of the aquarium's smaller creatures are contained in darkened, rather claustrophobic underground areas, full of tanks alive with all manner of marine life. This is where you can appreciate the immense variety of the world's seas and other aquatic habitats such as wetlands, Arctic Canada and the Amazon, all of which have dedicated display and educational areas.

Vancouver Art Gallery

Vancouver's principal art gallery is renowned for the paintings of Emily Carr, western Canada's most famous artist, as well as its contemporary art shows.

Classical conversion The staid exterior of the Vancouver Art Gallery belies the often startling modern art inside. Designed in 1911 by Francis Rattenbury (who was also responsible for many buildings in Victoria), the complex was originally created as the city's main courthouse, and preserves much of its early neoclassical grandeur and ornate decoration. Vancouver's leading modern architect, Arthur Erickson—who also designed the superb Museum of Anthropology (▷ 67)—remodeled much of the interior when the courthouse was transformed into the gallery in 1983.

Exhibitions only The gallery's emphasis in recent years has been on contemporary art, especially modern photography, and it owns wonderful images from Andreas Gursky, Cindy Sherman and Jenny Holzer, among others. However, only a very limited part of the permanent collection is exhibited at any one time, much of the gallery being given over to traveling exhibitions. Be certain these exhibitions are of interest to you, as the admission price is very high. If not, you can at least be sure of seeing many of the key works of Victoria-born Emily Carr (1871–1945), an artist who led a bohemian life, traveling widely in Europe and elsewhere, and whose vivid, almost surreal paintings, were heavily influenced by the landscapes and aboriginal cultures of western Canada.

THE BASICS

www.vanartgallery.bc.ca
✚ M4
✉ 750 Hornby Street at Robson Street
☎ Recorded information 604/662-4719
🕐 Mon, Wed, Fri, Sun, public hols 10–5.30; Tue, Thu 10–9
🍴 Gallery Café (▷ 39)
Ⓖ Granville
🚌 5, 50 to Robson Street or 2, 22, 32, 44 to Burrard Street
♿ Excellent
💲 Expensive; by donation (or free) Tue 5pm–9pm

HIGHLIGHTS

● Emily Carr paintings
● Photo-conceptual art
● Traveling exhibitions

DID YOU KNOW?

● Plans were announced in 2008 for a new venue for the Vancouver Art Gallery, in a waterside setting on False Creek's Plaza of Nations.

West End

Coal Harbour (left); charming Barclay Square (right and opposite)

THE BASICS

🗺 L3
🍴 Cafés on Denman and Davie streets
🚌 5 to Robson Street and Denman Street or 6 along Davie Street

Roedde House
🌐 www.roeddehouse.org
✉ 1415 Barclay Square
☎ 604/684-7040
🕐 Tue–Sat 1–5, Sun 2–4
♿ Good
💲 Inexpensive

HIGHLIGHTS

● Barclay Square
● Roedde House
● Gabriola Mansion
● Denman Street
● English Bay Beach

TIPS

● Denman Street is easily explored after visiting Stanley Park (▷ 26–27).
● West-facing English Bay Beach is a good place to watch the sun set.

The West End is a charming residential district, full of tree-lined streets and period houses, along with plenty of good shops, cafés and restaurants.

Prime land From virtually the moment white settlers occupied Vancouver, the West End district, between Stanley Park and Burrard and Thurlow streets in the east, was earmarked for exclusive residential use. The Canadian Pacific Railway owned and developed much of the land in the 1880s, building grand homes close to English Bay, some of which, such as Roedde House (open to the public) and others on and around Barclay Square, survive to this day. The area benefited from a decision by the city council in the 1950s to attract residents to the area, with the hope they would help keep the Downtown district alive. The plan worked, and much building now continues on the area's northern edge (Coal Harbour).

Street smart This has done little to affect the area's charm, which is generated by the genteel (sometimes bohemian) atmosphere, tree-lined streets, pretty houses and the air of easy-going affluence. Robson Street bisects the area, but the real appeal lies to its south, in the area bounded by Davie and Denman streets, which are lined with fun shops and great little cafés and restaurants, many with outside tables. There's not much to see in the area, but it is pleasant to wander, especially if you aim for English Bay Beach (▷ 32), where you can sit on the sand or relax in the pretty park to its rear.

More to See

CHRIST CHURCH CATHEDRAL
www.cathedral.vancouver.bc.ca
Vancouver's 1890s neo-Gothic
Anglican cathedral has inevitably been
dwarfed by Burrard Street's high-rise
buildings. Under its sandstone clad-
ding is a vast wooden frame made
from venerable Douglas firs. The
building hosts many cultural events,
as well as services. See the 32
stained-glass windows, especially the
William Morris window in the crypt.
✚ M4 ✉ 690 Burrard Street and West
Georgia ☎ 604/682-3848 🕔 Mon–Fri
9.30–4, Sat 9.30–4.30, Sun 1–5, longer hours
for services 🚇 Burrard 🚌 98 🎟 Free

COAL HARBOUR SEAWALK
The waterfront between Canada Place
and Stanley Park has been much
developed, with the arrival of many
attractively built and landscaped high-
rise condominiums. This pleasant
waterfront of parks, marinas and other
open spaces is linked for most of its
length by the Coal Harbour Seawalk.
The promenade offers a lovely walk,
plus restaurants and bar-cafés: It's
also a traffic-free way to reach Stanley
Park from the central Downtown area.
✚ L3 ✉ Coal Harbour Seawalk

ENGLISH BAY
You can see why so many people
want to live in the West End: Not only
is it bordered by Stanley Park, but in
English Bay it also has its own beach
and a wonderful watery outlook. The
bay is home to the 6m (20ft) high
Inukshuk Sculpture, an Inuit sign
of welcome and the symbol of the
2010 Vancouver Winter Olympics.
✚ J4 🚌 5, 6

MARINE BUILDING
Completed in 1930, the skyscraper
was intended to celebrate the city's
maritime links, its profile designed to
resemble a rocky headland and its
facade covered in art deco bas-reliefs
portraying fish, ships and other
marine motifs. The maritime theme
continues inside the lobby.
✚ M4 ✉ 355 Burrard Street and West
Hastings 🕔 Mon–Fri 8–6 🚇 Burrard
🚌 98 🎟 Free

The picturesque English Bay

*The Inukshuk Sculpture at
sunset, English Bay*

Downtown to Yaletown

This interesting walk takes you through Downtown to Yaletown, leaving you well-placed for visiting Granville Island.

DISTANCE: 3.2km (2 miles) **ALLOW:** 2 hours

START

CANADA PLACE
➕ M4 🚇 Waterfront 🚌 6, 44, 50

END

THE ROUNDHOUSE
➕ M5 🚌 C21, C23

❶ Walk up Burrard Street from Canada Place (▷ 24–25), passing the Marine Building (▷ 32) on your right. Turn left after Christ Church Cathedral (▷ 32) on West Georgia Street.

❽ From here, you can continue east on Davie Street to the waterfront, where you can pick up a ferry (▷ 118) that will take you to Science World (▷ 48) or Granville Island (▷ 65).

❷ On the right is the unmistakable Hotel Vancouver, resembling a French château, a city landmark and for decades Vancouver's most celebrated hotel (▷ 112).

❼ Explore the area, then find Davie Street and turn southeast to the corner with Pacific Boulevard and The Roundhouse (▷ 51).

❸ See the art displays and vast pendulum in the lobby of the bank building on the corner of West Georgia Street and Hornby Street (No. 885).

❻ Turn right on Homer Street, of little interest until you turn right on either Smithe Street or Nelson Street. South of here, on Mainland and Hamilton, is the heart of the trendy Yaletown district (▷ 50–51).

❹ Turn right on Hornby Street to Robson Street and the Vancouver Art Gallery (▷ 29). Perhaps have coffee in the Gallery Café (▷ 39) and explore the sunken Robson Square plaza.

❺ Turn left (east) on Robson Street and walk to Homer Street. In the distance you will see the distinctive BC Place Stadium, noted for its air-inflated dome. At Homer Street is the majestic Vancouver Public Library (▷ 52).

DOWNTOWN

WALK

Shopping

ARITZIA
www.aritzia.com
A trendy store where the staff are as hip as the smartly clad customers, who come for the latest women's clothes by top Canadian and international designers.
➕ L4 ✉ 1110 Robson Street at Thurlow ☎ 604/684-3251 🚇 Burrard 🚌 5

THE BAY
www.hbc.com
Canada's oldest and most famous department store is the outlet for the Hudson's Bay Company. You can still buy the company's celebrated "point" blankets, where each coloured stripe referred to the number of beaver pelts the blanket was worth in trade. Most of the shop is given over to classic department store goods.
➕ M4 ✉ 674 Granville Street at West Georgia ☎ 604/681-6211 🚇 Granville 🚌 5, 6, 15, 20, 50

BETSEY JOHNSON
www.betseyjohnson.com
One of the few international stores opened by this New York designer, known for her unconventional but feminine clothes.
➕ M4 ✉ 1033 Alberni Street at Burrard ☎ 604/488-0314 🚇 Burrard 🚌 2, 5, 22

BIRKS
www.birks.com
Birks is a nationwide chain that has had a presence in Vancouver since 1879. Most local couples getting married send their wedding list here for receiving good china, silver, glassware and fine jewelry.
➕ M4 ✉ 698 West Hastings Street ☎ 604/669-3333 🚇 Waterfront 🚌 10, 44

CASA DEL HABANO
www.havanahouse.com
One of the best of Vancouver's several fine cigar shops, with a walk-in humidor and many hundreds of items from the stock of Havana House, Cuba's largest supplier of cigars. You'll pay anything from a few to hundreds of dollars for individual cigars.

SHOPPING MALLS
Downtown has several major shopping malls. The biggest and best, with over 200 stores, is the Pacific Centre (☎ 604/688-7235; www.pacificcentre.com), stretching three blocks from Robson to Pender and from Howe to West Georgia streets. The emphasis is on clothes and shoes, but there are also plenty of more specialist stores. Farther afield, other key malls include the equally upscale but much smaller Sinclair Centre (▷ 35), The Landing (▷ 56) in Gastown and the more downscale Park Royal Shopping Centre in North Vancouver.

➕ M4 ✉ 402 Hornby Street ☎ 604/609-0511 🚇 Burrard 🚌 2, 5, 22

CHAPTERS
www.chapters.indigo.ca
An excellent central bookstore, with over 110,000 titles in stock, plus lots of national and international newspapers and magazines. The travel section is particularly good for maps and specialist guides to British Columbia.
➕ M4 ✉ 788 Robson Street at Howe ☎ 604/682-4066 or 1-888/648-0889 🚇 Granville 🚌 50 and other city center services

CLUB MONACO
www.clubmonaco.com
Club Monaco is a nationwide clothes chain with a similar style and clientele to Banana Republic. Lots of classic and contemporary clothes at mid-range prices for men and women. There are several outlets around the city.
➕ L4 ✉ 1034–1042 Robson Street at Jervis ☎ 604/687-8618 🚇 Burrard 🚌 5

EYES ON BURRARD
www.eyesonline.com
A big eyewear store known for its striking window displays. It has a long-established reputation for a large stock and for selling the latest styles from major names such as Paul Smith, Persol, Boucheron and others.
➕ M4 ✉ 775 Burrard Street at Robson ☎ 604/688-9521 🚇 Burrard 🚌 5

HMV
www.hmv.ca

A megastore on one of the busiest pedestrian junctions in Canada, never mind Vancouver. It sells a vast range of DVDs and games.
🔼 M4 ✉ 788 Burrard Street at Robson ☎ 604/669-2289 🚇 Burrard 🚌 5

HOLT RENFREW
www.holtrenfrew.com

Canada's most dazzling department store, and first port-of-call for men's and women's designer and other clothes from all the leading names. Also the Holts Salon & Spa and concession mini stores for Prada, Marni, Hugo Boss and others.
🔼 M4 ✉ 737 Dunsmuir Street at Granville ☎ 604/681-3121 🚇 Granville 🚌 50

LULULEMON
www.lululemon.com

A wide range of the latest yoga and sportswear for men and women from leading brands in a fun store that started life in Vancouver but now has outlets in Tokyo and beyond.
🔼 L4 ✉ 1148 Robson Street at Thurlow ☎ 604/681-3118 🚇 Burrard 🚌 5

MURCHIES
www.murchies.com

Murchies is an institution in Vancouver and Victoria (where it also has a store), selling a choice of over 40 types of coffee and 50 blends of tea.

There are several outlets around the city.
🔼 M4 ✉ 825 West Pender Street at Howe ☎ 604/669-0783 🚇 Burrard 🚌 19

ROOTS
www.roots.ca

Roots is a much-loved national chain, with distinctive street and sportswear, including coveted hoodies and retro Olympic jogging pants. As well as this showcase store, it has outlets across the city, including most major malls.
🔼 M4 ✉ 1001 Robson Street at Burrard ☎ 604/683-4305 🚇 Burrard 🚌 5, 50

SEARS
www.sears.ca

This US retail giant took over the vast store once occupied by Eatons, a

much-loved Canadian chain. It has a vast range of mid-range, mid-price items, and is especially good for clothing basics and items for the home. It also sells electrical goods, furniture, luggage and other travel accessories.
🔼 M4 ✉ 701 Granville Street at Robson ☎ 604/685-7112 🚇 Granville 🚌 5, 50

SINCLAIR CENTRE
www.sinclaircentre.com

A classy, upscale mall, pleasant to walk through even if you're not shopping, for it occupies four historic buildings, including the old Vancouver Post Office (1910) and Customs Examining Warehouse (1913). There is an excellent food court.
🔼 M4 ✉ 757 West Hastings Street ☎ 604/488-0017 🚇 Granville 🚌 5, 6, 15, 20, 44

TRUE VALUE VINTAGE
www.truevalue.com

There are plenty of secondhand clothing stores in Gastown (▷ 46–47) and in the funkier stretches of Main Street to the east, but True Value Vintage offers a big and conveniently located store full of clothes from as far back as the 1920s.
🔼 M4 ✉ 710 Robson Street at Granville ☎ 604/685-5403 🚇 Granville 🚌 5

Entertainment and Nightlife

900 WEST

www.fairmont.com/
hotelvancouver

The main bar of the
landmark Hotel
Vancouver (▷ 112) has
the look of a gentlemen's
club—all dark wood and
comfortable chairs—but
is surprisingly unstuffy,
and buzzes with guests,
shoppers and business-
people, especially from
5–7pm.

➕ M4 ✉ 900 West Georgia
Street at Hornby ☎ 604/
684-3131 ⓘ Mon–Thu, Sun
11.30am–midnight, Fri–Sat
11.30am–1am 🚇 Burrard
🚌 2, 5, 22, 32, C21, N22

LA BODEGA

www.labodegavancouver.com

A great Spanish bar that
has been around for
years, largely due to the
buzzy, laid-back approach,
good, cheap drinks, no-
nonsense tapas and other
more substantial meals.

➕ L5 ✉ 1277 Howe Street
at Davie ☎ 604/684-8815
ⓘ Mon–Thu 4.30–midnight,
Fri–Sun–midnight, Sat 5–
midnight, Sun 5pm–11pm
🚌 4, 6, 7, 10, 16, 17, C23,
N6, N9, N10, N17

CARDERO'S

www.carderos.com

A good stop on the
Coal Harbour waterfront
(▷ 32) for a drink out
on the patio in summer
or in the marine-themed
bar, with cozy sofas and
fireplace. Fine views
over the Burrard Inlet.
You can also eat well in
the restaurant.

➕ L3 ✉ 1583 Coal Harbour
Quay at Cardero ☎ 604/
669-7666 ⓘ Daily 11.30–11
🚌 19 along West Pender
Street or all services on West
Georgia Street

COMMODORE

www.commodoreballroom.
com

The city's favorite mid-
size venue for local and
international bands is a
converted art deco ball-
room which preserves
its original "sprung" floor.
Limited seating for diners
can be pre-booked.

➕ M4 ✉ 868 Granville
Street at Smithe ☎ 604/739-
4550 ⓘ Live music most
nights 🚇 Granville 🚌 5, 6,
8, 15, 20, N15

GINGER 62

www.ginger62.com

Dress up to fit in with this
club's ambience—amber
lighting, red and gold
paint, ottomans, couches

and an extravagant bar.
Asian fusion tapas, top
DJs and well-honed
clientele complete
the mix.

➕ L5 ✉ 1219 Granville
Street at Davie ☎ 604/
688-5494 ⓘ Fri–Sat 8pm–
3am; phone for details of
special nights 🚇 Yaletown-
Roundhouse 🚌 4, 6, 7, 10,
16, 20, 50, N9, N10, N17

MEDIA CLUB

www.themediaclub.ca

A small 150-person
capacity live music club,
with a large roster of
up-and-coming bands
of all musical persuasions,
plus the occasional
more prominent touring
performers.

➕ M5 ✉ 695 Cambie Street
at West Georgia ☎ 604/608-
2871 ⓘ Live music most
nights 🚇 Stadium 🚌 15,
N15, N24

O'DOULS

www.odoulsrestaurant.com

A smart hotel bar where
you can hear smooth live
jazz most nights, accom-
panied by excellent food
and drink.

➕ L4 ✉ 1300 Robson Street
at Jervis ☎ 604/661-1400
ⓘ Mon–Sat 7am–1am, Sun
7am–midnight 🚇 Burrard
🚌 5, N6

PLAZA CLUB

www.plazaclub.net

One of Granville's many
former cinemas, the
Plaza is now a central
mid-size venue that is
low on atmosphere but
regularly presents decent

touring bands (with a weekly showcase for local performers). Club nights offer mainstream dance music, with popular theme nights.

➕ M4 ✉ 881 Granville Street at Robson ☎ 604/646-0064 🕐 Daily 9pm–3am 🚇 Granville 🚌 All city center buses

QUEEN ELIZABETH THEATRE

www.city.vancouver.bc.ca/theatres

This 2,900-seat venue is the main auditorium for Vancouver's mainstream performing arts, hosting city and touring orchestras, opera companies, dance companies, theater productions and more.

➕ M4 ✉ 600 Hamilton Street at Dunsmuir ☎ Information 604/665-3050 🚇 Stadium 🚌 5, 6, 8, 20, N19, N24

THE RAILWAY CLUB

www.therailwayclub.com

Vancouver's best small venue (capacity 175), and a long-time favorite—it's been in business since the 1930s. Known for its friendly staff, no-nonsense pub atmosphere, and for championing a range of live music.

➕ M4 ✉ 579 Dunsmuir Street at Seymour ☎ 604/681-1625 🕐 Mon–Thu noon–2am, Fri noon–3am, Sat 2pm–3am, Sun 4pm–midnight 🚇 Granville 🚌 4, 6, 7, 8, 10, 16, 20, 50, N6, N8, N9, N10, N15, N20

RED ROOM ON RICHARDS

www.redroomonrichards.com

A well-located mid-size (400 capacity) club and venue for dancing and live music.

➕ M4 ✉ 398 Richards Street at West Cordova ☎ 604/687-5007 🕐 Mon–Thu, Sun 9pm–2am, Fri–Sat 9pm–3am 🚇 Waterfront 🚌 4, 7, 8, 50

THE ROXY

www.roxyvan.com

A fun club of the old school, with four bars and a clientele of teens, college students, visitors and locals. Live bands (or house band) some nights, plus dance music.

➕ M5 ✉ 932 Granville Street at Nelson ☎ 604/331-7999 🕐 Daily 7pm–3am 🚇 Waterfront 🚌 4, 50

OUTDOOR THEATER

Two of Vancouver's best-loved summer events take place outdoors—weather allowing. The Malkin Bowl arena in Stanley Park hosts Theatre Under the Stars (☎ 604/734-1917; www.tuts.ca, mid-Jul to mid-Aug), which usually involves two popular lightweight productions. Bard on the Beach (☎ Box office 604/739-0559; www.bardonthebeach.org, Jun–end Sep) takes place in a large tent in Vanier Park overlooking English Bay. Two Shakespeare plays are usually performed.

VANCOUVER PLAYHOUSE THEATRE COMPANY

www.vancouverplayhouse.com

The large, purpose-built 700-seat Vancouver Playhouse (part of the Queen Elizabeth complex) is home to Vancouver's leading theater company.

➕ M4 ✉ Corner of Hamilton and Dunsmuir streets ☎ 604/873-3311 🚇 Stadium 🚌 5, 6, 8, 20, N19, N24

VANCOUVER SYMPHONY ORCHESTRA

www.vancouversymphony.ca
www.city.vancouver.bc.ca/theatres

Vancouver's highly respected showpiece symphony orchestra usually performs at the Chan Centre or the Orpheum. The latter is one of the city's finest theaters.

➕ M4 🎭 Orpheum Theatre, 884 Granville Street at Smithe ☎ 604/876-3434 🚇 Granville 🚌 4, 6, 7 and city center buses

THE YALE

www.theyale.ca

The key venue (capacity 300) in the city for hard-core rock, blues and old-style R&B. Live music most nights, including international names.

➕ L5 ✉ 1300 Granville Street at Drake ☎ 604/681-9253 🕐 Live music most nights 🚇 Yaletown-Roundhouse 🚌 4, 6, 7, 8, 10, 16, 20, 50, N9, N10, N17, N15

Restaurants

PRICES

Prices are approximate, based on a 3-course meal for one person.
$$$ over $40
$$ $20–$40
$ under $20

BIN 941 ($)
www.bin941.com
Cramped and noisy, but popular and busy, this hole-in-the-wall wine bar has spawned many imitators. The bite-size "tapatizers" are part of the appeal, along with the well-chosen wines and animated atmosphere.
🕂 L5 ✉ 941 Davie Street at Hornby ☎ 604/683-1246 🕐 Mon–Sat 5pm–1.30am, Sun 5pm–midnight 🚌 6

CINCIN ($$)
www.cincin.net
Long a fixture on Robson Street, upscale but informal CinCin has become almost an institution. The big open dining room is warm and welcoming, the Italian food is rich and generally accomplished, and the atmosphere is buzzy. Prices can be high, but not excessive, given the location.
🕂 L4 ✉ 1154 Robson Street at Thurlow ☎ 604/688-7338 🕐 Mon–Fri 11.30am–11pm, Sat 9am–10.30pm 🚌 Burrard 🚌 5

LE CROCODILE ($$$)
www.lecrocodilerestaurant.com
Chef Michel Jacob's Alsace-influenced cuisine has set the pace for French food in Vancouver since 1983. The dining room is in an unassuming location, but inside feels like an authentic French bistro. Food sticks to French classics, with the odd local West Coast influence.
🕂 M4 ✉ 100-909 Burrard Street, entrance on Smithe Street ☎ 604/669-4298 🕐 Mon–Fri 11.30–2, 5.30–10, Sat 5.30–10.30 🚌 Granville 🚌 2, 4, 7, 10, 16, 17, 22, 32, 44

DELILAH'S ($$)
www.delilahs.ca
Delilah's has been a fun, decadent and deliberately

IZAKAYA

Vancouver's pan-Pacific links have made first Chinese and latterly Japanese food popular. Trends from Japan quickly catch on, including one of the latest, *izakaya*, which means "eat-drink place." These are small, informal and inexpensive establishments, often with an open kitchen and no reservations, serving tapas-like Japanese dishes (and perhaps Korean, Chinese and some Western ones as well). Good examples include Hapa Izakaya (✉ 1479 Robson Street near Broughton ☎ 604/689-4272; www.hapaizakaya.com) and Guu (✉ 838 Thurlow Street ☎ 604/685-8817; www.guu-izakaya.com).

---

kitsch fixture of the West End for over 20 years. Dine on inexpensive tapas or the French-influenced main courses, perhaps preceded by one of the restaurant's famous martinis, while enjoying the velvet banquettes, hand-painted cherubim and other decorative flourishes.
🕂 K4 ✉ 1789 Comox Street near Denman ☎ 604/687-3424 🕐 Daily 5pm–10 or later 🚌 5, 6

DIVA AT THE MET ($$$)
www.metropolitan.com
The restaurant of the Metropolitan Hotel has established a good (if sometimes erratic) reputation of its own over the years, separate from the hotel. The sophisticated food can be excellent (fish and seafood in particular) and the modern dining room (splashy art aside) is sleek and modern. Dress up to be sure of fitting in.
🕂 M4 ✉ 645 Howe Street at Dunsmuir ☎ 604/602-7788 🕐 Daily 7–2.30, 5.30–10.30 🚌 Granville 🚌 5, 6, 20, 50 and all other city services

EARLS ($–$$)
If the plethora of choice in Downtown, or the prices, become too much, you can do a lot worse than Earls, part of a long-established chain with a simple,

non-chain formula: pleasant, modern dining rooms; mid-range prices; friendly service; first-rate ingredients; and excellent food that offers a little from Italian, Asian, French and other cuisines.

L4 ✉ 710 Robson Street at Bute ☎ 604/669-0020 Ⓘ Daily 11.30am–1am Ⓠ Burrard 🚌 5

FISH HOUSE AT STANLEY PARK ($$)

www.fishhousestanleypark. com

A pretty leafy setting on the fringe of Stanley Park, an attractive white-clap board building and some superlative fish and seafood make this a popular destination for West End locals. The dining rooms, in green and white, and offset by dark wood, have a colonial, club-like air. Full meals and an excellent afternoon tea.

K3 ✉ 8901 Stanley Park Drive at Lagoon Drive ☎ 604/681 7275 Ⓘ Daily 11 or 11.30–10 🚌 6

GALLERY CAFÉ ($)

www.vanartgallery.bc.ca

The bright, modern café of the Vancouver Art Gallery is one of the best places in Downtown for lunch, especially in summer, when you can sit outside on the big terrace. You wait in line for the food, which is more adventurous than most cafeteria fare, with daily specials, soups,

salads, sandwiches and a good variety of light meals.

M4 ✉ 750 Hornby Street at Robson ☎ 604/688-2233 Ⓘ Mon, Wed, Fri–Sat 9–5.30; Tue, Thu 9–9, Sun 10–5 Ⓠ Burrard 🚌 5

LE GAVROCHE ($$$)

www.legavroche.ca

The contemporary French food (with a West Coast twist) at Le Gavroche (opened in an historic West End town house in 1979), is almost as good as Le Crocodile, but the romantic dining room sets it apart, with its mirrors,

CHAIN RESTAURANTS

Vancouver has many excellent chains offering quality food. The best-known is family-friendly White Spot (www. whitespot.ca), which serves burgers, pastas and fabulous desserts. The most convenient Downtown branch is 580 West Georgia Street (☎ 604/ 662-3066). Joey's (visit www. joeysmedgrill.com for locations) and Milestones (www.milestonesrestaurants. com) are similar, and aimed at a younger clientele. Milestones in the West End (✉ 1210 Denman Street ☎ 604/662-3431), is near English Bay Beach. Other chains include Flying Wedge (www.flyingwedge.com) for gourmet pizza and Soupspoons (www.soupspoons.com) for home-made soups.

paintings, open fireplace and dark-painted walls.

L3 ✉ 1616 Alberni Street at Bidwell ☎ 604/685-3924 Ⓘ Daily 5.30pm–late 🚌 5, 19

IL GIARDINO DI UMBERTO ($$–$$$)

www.umberto.com

Umberto Menghi has been serving great modern Italian food at this homey villa-like town house and lovely vine-covered terrace on the edge of Yaletown since 1973. Lunch sees many business customers, and evenings a smart but relaxed crowd. The dishes are more exotic than you'd find in Italy (reindeer loin, ostrich in wild berry sauce) but are expertly prepared in convivial surroundings.

L5 ✉ 1382 Hornby Street at Pacific Boulevard ☎ 604/ 669-2422 Ⓘ Mon–Fri 11.30am–midnight, Sat 5.30pm–midnight Ⓠ Stadium 🚌 15

IMPERIAL ($$$)

www.imperialrest.com

Offers an elegant dining experience in the historic Marine Building (▷ 32). The 300-seat dining room—all white walls, deep blue carpets and crisp table linen—has windows down one side, providing a panoramic accompaniment to fine Cantonese-influenced fish, seafood and other dishes, including dim sum.

The set menus are generally good value.
⊞ M4 ⊠ Marine Building, 355 Burrard Street ☎ 604/688-8191 ⚫ Daily 10.30–10.30 Ⓜ Burrard 🚌 5, 19, 22

KIRIN MANDARIN ($$)

www.kirinrestaurant.com
One of the first smart, so-called "white-tablecloth" Chinese restaurants in Downtown, Kirin has a spacious, modern and elegant dining room. The sophisticated food embraces several regional cuisines, including Cantonese and Sichuan.
⊞ L4 ⊠ 1166 Alberni Street at Bute ☎ 604/682-8833 ⚫ Daily 11–2.30, 5–10.30 (opens 10am Sun) Ⓜ Burrard 🚌 5

LIFT BAR & GRILL ($$)

www.liftbarandgrill.com
A stone's throw from Cardero's (▷ 36) and with the same wonderful waterfront views. The $8-million dining room, with its vast glass walls, is modern and sleek, though the West Coast food is less striking. Book ahead in summer.
⊞ L3 ⊠ 333 Menchions Mews at Bayshore Drive ☎ 604/689-5438 ⚫ Mon–Fri 11.30am–midnight, Sat–Sun 11am–midnight 🚌 5 then 10-minute walk

LOLITA'S ($)

www.lolitasrestaurant.com
One look at the funky, bright dining room gives you an idea of what to expect from Lolita's, a fun and unfussy neighborhood café-restaurant where no dressing up is required and the mostly Mexican food is filling and inexpensive. It's also good for a late-night drink.
⊞ L4 ⊠ 1326 Davie Street at Jervis ☎ 604/696-9996 ⚫ Mon–Thu 4.30pm–2am, Fri–Sun 3pm–2am 🚌 6

PROSPECT POINT CAFÉ ($)

www.prospectpoint.ca
There is nothing fancy about this café, but its position midway around the Seawall in Stanley Park, and the magnificent views from the terrace, make it an obvious stop for walkers and bicyclists. It can get busy in summer and on weekends.
⊞ K1 ⊠ Prospect Point, Stanley Park Drive, Stanley Park ☎ 604/669-2737 ⚫ Daily 9–8; more formal lunches 11.30–4 🚌 19

VEGGIE OPTIONS

Most restaurants in Vancouver offer vegetarian or vegan menu choices. Chinese and other Asian restaurants in particular offer good non-meat and non-fish dishes, especially if you go for dim sum. Alternatively, head for The Naam (▷ 76) in Kitsilano—the city's foremost health-food and vegetarian restaurant since 1968.

RAINCITY GRILL ($$)

www.raincitygrill.com
A showcase since 1990 for West Coast cooking and the best, locally sourced (and often organic) ingredients. Wine, too, is often local, with over 100 wines by the glass. The romantic candlelit dining room of this delightful restaurant overlooks English Bay.
⊞ K4 ⊠ 1193 Denman Street at Davie ☎ 604/685-7337 ⚫ Mon–Fri 11.30–2, 5–10, Sat–Sun 10.30–2, 5–10 🚌 5, 6

SEQUOIA GRILL AT THE TEAHOUSE ($$)

www.vancouverdine.com
Bright, modern bistro (in a former barracks from 1928) at panoramic Ferguson Point in Stanley Park. The seasonal West Coast menu (fish, seafood, pastas, steaks) is not as good as the views. You need to book ahead.
⊞ J2 ⊠ Ferguson Point, Stanley Park ☎ 604/669-3281 ⚫ Mon–Sat 11.30–2, 5–10, Sun 10.30–3, 5–10 🚌 5

TEMPLETON ($–$$)

www.thetempleton.com
A fun 1950s-style diner, all chrome and vinyl, but the diner-style food is modern and with a nod to healthy eating. Vegetarian options are available and the big breakfasts are superb.
⊞ L5 ⊠ 1087 Granville Street at Helmcken ☎ 604/685-4612 ⚫ Daily 9am–11pm or later 🚌 4, 6, 7, 10, 16

East Vancouver embraces historic Gastown, the heart of the original city, and two fascinating and contrasting enclaves: Chinatown, a vibrant world apart, and Yaletown, a trendy and revitalized warehouse district.

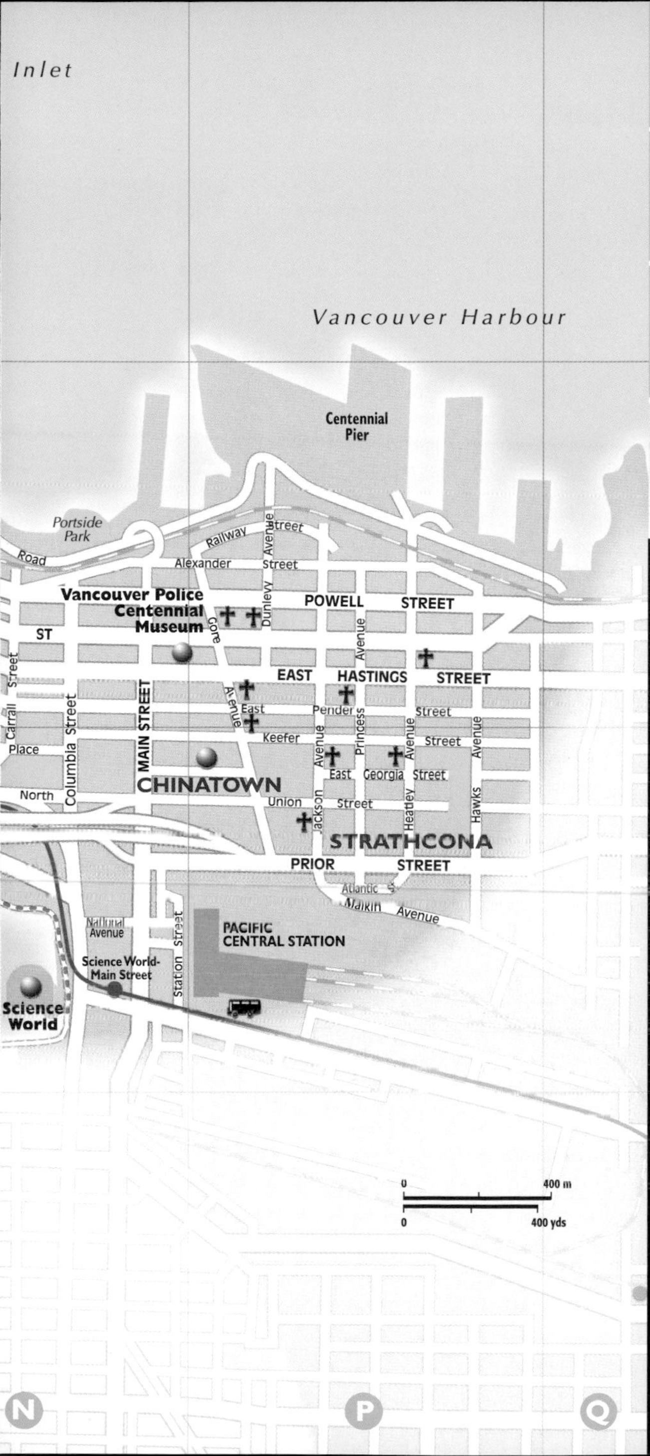

Inlet

Vancouver Harbour

Centennial
Pier

*Portside
Park*

Railway

Alexander   Street

Street

Dunlevy   Avenue

Core

POWELL   STREET

**Vancouver Police
Centennial
Museum**

ST

Avenue

EAST   HASTINGS   STREET

Carrall   Street

Columbia Street

MAIN STREET

Avenue

East

Pender

Keefer

Princess

Street

Street

Avenue

Place

East   Georgia   Street

Hawks   Avenue

North

Heatley

CHINATOWN

Union   Street

Jackson   Street

STRATHCONA

PRIOR   STREET

Atlantic

Malkin   Avenue

*National
Avenue*

Station Street

**PACIFIC
CENTRAL STATION**

Science World-
Main Street

**Science
World**

0		400 m
0		400 yds

N   P   Q

Chinatown

Chinatown is a city apart, full of tiny streets, specialist shops, colorful night markets, busy restaurants and the buzz of Chinese conversation.

Close community Chinatown's 100,000-plus inhabitants make up one of the largest Chinese communities outside the Far East, comparable to the similar communities in New York and San Francisco. They also make up the city's largest and oldest ethnic group after those of European extraction. Many of their ancestors crossed the Pacific in 1858 during the British Columbian gold rush, or shortly afterward, to help build the Canadian Pacific Railway. Although marginalized (and often discriminated against) for decades, the area's clan associations and societies helped newcomers forge a life and create a self-sustaining community.

Clockwise from left: The distinctive skyline of Chinatown; for an authentic experience of Chinese culture visit one of the many herbalists and peruse the vast selection of remedies; the tranquil Dr. Sun Yat-Sen Garden and one of its inhabitants; learn about the cultural heritage of Vancouver's Chinese immigrants

百年风云

THE BASICS

✚ P5
🚇 Stadium
🚌 10, 16, 20
♿ Very good

Dr. Sun Yat-Sen Garden
www.vancouverchinese garden.com
✉ 578 Carrall Street at Pender
☎ 604/662 3207
🕐 Mid-Jun to end Aug daily 9.30–7; May to mid-Jun, Sep daily 10–6; Oct–end Apr daily 10–4.30
🍴 Cafés ($)
✋ Moderate
❓ Free 45-minute guided tours every half-hour (4–8pm daily)

Chinese Cultural Centre
✉ 555 Columbia Street
☎ 604/658-8880 or 604/ 658-8850
🕐 Tue–Sun 11–5
🍴 Cafés ($)
✋ Inexpensive (free Tue)
❓ Tours and workshops available (inexpensive)

The Chinese Cultural Centre Museum offers insights into the district and its history.

Garden sanctuary The main sight is the Dr. Sun Yat-Sen Garden, named after the founder of the Chinese Republic and built with Chinese help for Expo'86 at a cost of $5.3 million. It was the first classical-style Chinese garden built in the West. Ordered and tranquil within its walls, it provides a marked contrast to the busy streets (notably Pender and Keefer from Abbott and Main to Gore), where everything—buildings, shops, signs— is authentically Chinese. Visit the Sam Kee Building (1913) at 8 West Pender Street (on the corner of Carrall), which at 1.8m (2 yards) wide is one of the world's narrowest houses, but also leave time to explore the shops, especially the herbalists, with their strange assortment of cures.

Gastown

HIGHLIGHTS

● Water Street
● Vancouver Police
Centennial Museum (▷ 52)
● Maple Tree Square
● Steam Clock
● The Landing (▷ 56)
● Inuit Gallery (▷ 55)

TIP

● Gastown becomes busy, so arrive early to beat the crowds.

Vancouver's original heart is now a rejuvenated area of visitor-filled streets, specialist stores and appealing cafés, bars and restaurants.

Boozy beginnings Gastown takes its name from the larger-than-life "Gassy" Jack Deighton, a hard-living publican who, in the 1860s, opened a bar to serve loggers clearing what was then little more than virgin forest on the banks of the Burrard Inlet. A ramshackle community— Gassy's Town—grew up and was renamed Granville in 1869 (population 400), only to burn to the ground during the Great Fire of 1886, three months after having been rechristened "Vancouver." "Gassy" Jack is commemorated by a statue in Maple Tree Square, at the heart of the small grid of Victorian-era streets.

Clockwise from left: The namesake of Gastown, "Gassy" Jack; the quirky steam-powered clock on Water Street; many of the galleries in this district display native artwork; Gastown has a host of off-beat shops and cafés set against a historic backdrop, perfect for a leisurely stroll

Water Street In the second half of the 20th century, Vancouver began to expand to the west and Gastown's importance declined. As a result, much of the area became run down, but over the last two decades it has been revived. For a few years after renovation began, the area remained rather soulless, but recently more interesting shops, galleries, nightspots and restaurants have begun to open. There are few "sights" as such, and the area is best seen on a walking tour (▷ 54).

The main points of interest are the Police Museum (▷ 52) and Steam Clock, built in 1977 on Water Street, the area's main thoroughfare, as a miniature version of London's Big Ben. Also on Water Street is The Landing (▷ 56), an upscale mall, but be sure to explore beyond this street, especially as Gastown's regeneration reaches gradually farther east.

THE BASICS

✚ N4
🍴 Incendio (▷ 60), Steamworks (▷ 58), Water Street Café (▷ 60)
Ⓦ Waterfront
🚌 4, 6, 7, 8
♿ Good

Science World

Science World brings science alive with interactive displays

THE BASICS

www.scienceworld.bc.ca

➕ N5

✉ 1455 Québec Street at Termial Avenue

☎ 604/443-7440. Recorded information 604/443-7443

🕐 Mon–Fri 10–5, Sat–Sun 10–6

🍴 White Spot ($) on site

🚇 Main Street-Science World

🚌 3

♿ Very good

💰 Expensive. Omnimax moderate. Combined tickets available

HIGHLIGHTS

● Omnimax cinema
● Hands-on displays

TIPS

● Best reached by SkyTrain from Downtown.
● From Granville Island (▷ 65) and Yaletown (▷ 50–51), a fun way to reach Science World is by ferry (▷ 118).

Children will love the many innovative hands-on displays in Science World, which is housed in one of Vancouver's most striking contemporary buildings.

Crowd-pleaser Not everything built for Expo'86, Vancouver's world trade fair, survived. One building that did—luckily—is Buckminster Fuller's dazzling mirror-covered geodesic dome (or the "silver golf ball," as locals call it), a suitably futuristic setting for this large and wide-ranging collection of often crazy and innovative exhibits and interactive displays devoted to all branches of science. Ideal for children, and a good rainy-day choice, it has plenty of science shows full of bangs, flashes and other crowd-pleasing effects to supplement the sophisticated and imaginative displays.

Something for all These displays are ranged across two levels, and embrace technology, natural history and most other science-related areas. Among other things, there are exhibits devoted to sustainability and the environment, a water course, a giant maze, plus the chance to search for gold, blow square bubbles, see how a beehive works and play tunes by walking on a giant keyboard. There is also a dedicated area for children under six, a 400-seat Omnimax cinema (on level three of the building) showing large-screen documentaries, and a restaurant for decent food at good prices. Be warned that the complex becomes extremely busy—and occasionally hectic—despite its size, especially around 2pm and during school terms, when it is popular with large school groups.

The Vancouver Lookout (right) offers breathtaking views of the city (left)

Vancouver Lookout

The ride to this skyscraper's observation gallery is one of Vancouver's most exhilarating and the far-reaching view from the top is one of the best in the city.

Ticket to ride You look up from below. Is that really a pair of glass elevators on the outside of a skyscraper? Yes, it is, and the so-called SkyLift offers a breathtaking—if stomach-churning—one-minute ride of 167m (548ft) from ground level to the Vancouver Lookout, the observation platform at the top of the Harbour Centre Building. Opened in 1977 by Neil Armstrong, the first man on the moon, this building was the highest in the city for many years, and acquired the nickname "The Hamburger," after its bulging upper floors.

Perfect panorama Choose a fine day, and the 360-degree view from the top is superb, and provides an interesting counterpoint to the panorama from the top of Grouse Mountain (▷ 84). Here, the vista looks across the older, low-rise area of eastern Vancouver. But it also extends miles south, to the peaks of Washington State across the United States border, and to Vancouver Island and the wild uplands of North Vancouver.

Food with a view Information boards dotted around the Lookout identify landmarks on the city skyline, backed up by multimedia displays. Period photographs illustrate how the city has changed. There are occasional free tours. If you book a table at the revolving restaurant, the entry fee is waived.

THE BASICS

www.vancouverlookout.com

✚ M4

✉ 555 West Hastings Street at Seymour

☎ 604/689-0421

🕐 May to mid-Oct daily 8.30am–10.30pm; mid-Oct to end Apr daily 9–9

🍽 Top of Vancouver Revolving Restaurant ($$)

🚇 Waterfront

🚌 4, 6, 7, 8, 50

♿ Very good

💰 Moderate

HIGHLIGHTS

● SkyLift ride
● The views
● Period photographs

TIPS

● The Vancouver Lookout is best seen en route between Canada Place and Gastown.
● Tickets are valid all day. Come early to avoid the crowds and/or late to catch the sunset.

Yaletown

HIGHLIGHTS

● Specialist shops
(▷ 55–56)
● Yaletown Brewing
Company (▷ 58)
● The Roundhouse

TIP

● Use ferries (▷ 118) to
make the journey to and
from Granville Island or
Science World.

Yaletown is an old warehouse district that, in the last 10 years, has been transformed into a tempting enclave of trendy shops, bars, cafés and restaurants.

Transformation Most major cities have an area like Yaletown, a former semi-industrial district whose cheap rents and old buildings first attract artists, artisans and design and media businesses, before the area is transformed into a more affluent enclave of sassy boutiques, restaurants and converted lofts and other apartments.

Lawless The area is a grid of streets focused on Homer, Hamilton and Mainland between Drake and Smithe. It takes its name from the Canadian Pacific Railway (CPR) workers who settled here in the 1880s, having moved west with the railway

Yaletown has enjoyed redevelopment in recent years, preserving its industrial roots while attracting trendy bars and eateries to serve both its growing residential population and those on the tourist trail

from Yale, 180km (112 miles) away. Then, it reputedly had more bars per acre than anywhere else in the world, and was so lawless that even the Mounties stayed away. Something of its past can be glimpsed in the rails embedded in many streets, and at The Roundhouse, a community arts center, and once a shed for turning locomotives. One of the engines, which hauled the first passenger train into the city in 1887, can still be seen.

New growth Today Yaletown is an attractive area to explore but beyond its little grid of streets this is still a rather uninspiring part of the city. The old warehouse architecture and wide boardwalks survive, though to the south ranks of new high-rise apartment blocks are taking root near Yaletown Landing, where a good way to move on is by using the quay's tiny ferries.

THE BASICS

✚ M5
🍴 Many local cafés
🚇 Yaletown-Roundhouse (Canada Line due to open Nov 2009)
🚌 1, 6, 7, 10, 16, 17
♿ Roundhouse good. Yaletown generally poor

The Roundhouse
✉ Roundhouse Mews at Davie Street and Pacific Boulevard
☎ 604/713-1800
🕐 Hours vary
💷 Free

More to See

VANCOUVER POLICE CENTENNIAL MUSEUM

www.vancouverpolicemuseum.ca

Just two blocks from Chinatown, this fascinating little museum is housed in the old Coroner's Court Building, and contains displays relating to the often bizarre history of Vancouver's police force. You can see the autopsy room, with preserved body parts; a police cell; and a radio room. There are also thematic displays devoted to gambling, counterfeiting, weapons seized from criminals and more. Take a taxi to the museum, as the surroundings are unpleasant.

➕ N4 ✉ 240 East Cordova Street ☎ 604/665-3346 🕐 Mon–Sat 9–5 🚌 4, 7
✋ Inexpensive

VANCOUVER PUBLIC LIBRARY

www.vpl.ca

Vancouver's stunning library is an architectural tour de force; a latter-day Colosseum (though architect Moshe Safdie apparently denies the resemblance was intentional) that cost $100 million, making it the most expensive public project in the city's history when it opened in 1995. It's worth stepping inside the building, either to use it or to ride the escalators to the upper floors for some fine views. Library Square around the building (and the glass atrium at the entrance) is an attractive plaza of cafés, stores and public spaces.

➕ M5 ✉ 350 West Georgia Street at Robson and Homer ☎ 604/331-3603
🕐 Mon–Thu 10–9, Fri–Sat 10–6, Sun 12–5

WATERFRONT STATION

When it was built in 1915, this imposing neoclassical building was the terminus of the Canadian Pacific Railway, the transcontinental line that changed Vancouver's destiny and helped forge Canada as a country (▷ 125). Today, it contains offices and bland shops and cafés. Also here is the entrance to the Waterfront SkyTrain station, a transit point between SkyTrain and the SeaBus terminal (▷ 87).

➕ N4 ✉ 601 West Cordova Street at Granville

The grand entrance of Waterfront Station (above). A decorative stained-glass window at the Vancouver Police Centennial Museum (opposite)

The glass atrium of the Vancouver Public Library (right)

A Stroll around Gastown

You can extend this easy walk around Vancouver's rejuvenated historic district to include the streets and sights of Chinatown.

DISTANCE: 1km (0.6 miles) to Maple Tree Square   **ALLOW:** 2 hours

START

CANADA PLACE
✚ M4 🚇 Waterfront 🚌 6, 44, 50

END

MAPLE TREE SQUARE
✚ N4 🚌 4, 7, 8, 50

① From the fountain in front of Canada Place (▷ 24–25), adorned with the flags of Canada's provinces and territories, walk east (left), following Howe Street to West Cordova Street.

② Turn left down West Cordova Street past Waterfront Station (▷ 52) on your left. If it's a nice day, visit the Vancouver Lookout (▷ 49), almost opposite the station, for wonderful views of the city.

③ At the junction of West Cordova Street and Richards Street, the start of Gastown, take the left fork, Water Street, the area's main thoroughfare.

④ Walk down Water Street, passing The Landing period building (▷ 56) on your left (No. 375), built partly on the proceeds of the 1896 Klondike Gold Rush.

⑧ It is an easy, but unpleasant three-block walk (perhaps take a cab) south on Carrall Street from Maple Tree Square to East Pender Street for the Sam Kee Building (▷ 45) and Dr. Sun Yat-Sen Garden (▷ 45). Chinatown's core is two blocks east on Keefer Street.

⑦ Nearby, at 2 Water Street, see the Byrnes Block (1886), Vancouver's oldest building on its original site. Also see pretty Trounce Alley, Gaoler's Mews and Blood Alley just to the south.

⑥ At the end of Water Street is Maple Tree Square, with a statue of "Gassy" Jack Deighton, after whom Gastown is named (▷ 46–47).

⑤ At the junction of Water Street and Cambie Street is the Steam Clock (▷ 47). Leave Water Street to explore the stores and galleries of First Nations art on Cambie and Abbott streets.

Shopping

ATOMIC MODEL
www.atomicmodel.com
A hip, popular Yaletown store selling the latest designer clothes and accessories.
➕ M5 ✉ 1036 Mainland Street ☎ 604/688-9989 Ⓜ Yaletown-Roundhouse 🚌 C23

CHINATOWN NIGHT MARKET
www.vcma.shawbiz.ca
This is a lively market, with booths, tables and stalls selling food, fake goods and trinkets, spilling over two buzzing city blocks around Keefer and Pender streets. Take a taxi from Downtown.
➕ P5 ✉ 100–200 Keefer Street ☎ 604/682-8998 🔆 Mid-May to mid-Sep Fri-Sun from 6.30pm 🚌 4, 7, 8

CHINTZ
www.chintz.com
One of the largest of Yaletown's many design and homeware stores. Features a wide range of fabrics, furniture and other products.
➕ M5 ✉ 950 Homer Street ☎ 604/689-2022 Ⓜ Yaletown-Roundhouse 🚌 3

COASTAL PEOPLES FINE ARTS GALLERY
www.coastalpeoples.com
A bright, modern Yaletown gallery dealing in First Nations arts, it sells top-price gold, silver and other jewelry, plus small totems, carvings, prints, paintings

and Inuit sculpture. There is a Gastown outlet at 312 Water Street (tel 604/684-9222).
➕ M5 ✉ 1024 Mainland Street ☎ 604/685-9298 or 1-888/686-9298 Ⓜ Yaletown-Roundhouse 🚌 C23

THE CROSS
www.thecrossdesign.com
A large design and homeware store in a 1914 heritage building. A good source of fun gifts, home accessories and also larger pieces of furniture.
➕ M5 ✉ 1198 Homer Street at Davie ☎ 604/689-2900 or 1-877/689-2902 Ⓜ Yaletown-Roundhouse 🚌 15

DELUXE JUNK
www.deluxejunk.com
Junk by name and junk by nature—many of the secondhand clothes here

--- **ANTIQUES** ---
"Antique Row," the traditional heart of the antiques trade, lies on Main Street between 16th and 25th avenues south of King Edward Avenue. This is part of so-called SoMa (▷ 71), an emerging shopping district, but it remains a good area to browse. Good stores include Legends (✉ 4366 Main Street ☎ 604/875-0621), for retro clothes and jewelry, and Deeler's Antiques (4391 Main Street, ☎ 604/879-3394), a warren of corridors full of small specialist dealers.

are virtually worthless, but there are a few gems.
➕ N4 ✉ 310 West Cordova Street at Cambie ☎ 604/685-4871 Ⓜ Waterfront 🚌 6, 7, 8, 10, 20, 50

IMAGES FOR A CANADIAN HERITAGE
www.imagesforcanada.com
Even if you don't want to buy (prices are high), come to this Gastown gallery to admire some of Canada's finest Inuit and other Pacific Northwest First Nations art and items.
➕ N4 ✉ 164 Water Street ☎ 604/685-7046 Ⓜ Waterfront 🚌 4, 7, 8, 10, 16, 20, 50

INFORM INTERIORS
www.informinteriors.com
A Gastown store that showcases the best in contemporary homeware, including work from Philippe Starck, Mies van de Rohe, Charles Eames and owner-designer Niels Bendtsen, best known for his "Ribbon Chair."
➕ N4 ✉ 50 and 97 Water Street at Abbott ☎ 604/682-3868 Ⓜ Waterfront 🚌 4, 7, 8, 10, 16, 20, 50

INUIT GALLERY OF VANCOUVER
www.inuit.com
Long-established gallery similar to Images for a Canadian Heritage (▷ above). Sells the best Inuit art, from masks, prints and painted chests to jewelry and wood, bone and other sculpture.

N4   206 Cambie Street
☎ 604/688-7323 or 1-888/
615-8399   Waterfront
4, 7, 8, 10, 16, 20, 50

JADE
www.jademine.com
It may look like a souvenir store, but it sells a superb range of items made from jade. Much comes from the Polar Mine in northern British Columbia, considered the source of the world's best jade.
N4   4-375 Water Street   ☎ 604/687-5233
Waterfront   4, 7, 8, 10, 16, 20, 50

JOHN FLUEVOG
www.fluevog.com
This local cult shoemaker has been in business for more than 20 years and retains a street-cred image that has made him a darling of the fashion crowd. Second outlet at 837 Granville Street between Robson and Smithe.
N4   65 Water Street at Abbott   ☎ 604/688-6228
Waterfront   4, 7, 8, 10, 16, 20, 50

THE LANDING
www.the-landing.com
The Landing (1905) was one of Gastown's main warehouses, but has been converted into a small mall with designer outlets, souvenir stores, cafés and restaurants.
N4   375 Water Street   ☎ 604/453-5050
Waterfront   4, 7, 8, 10, 16, 20, 50

MINTAGE VINTAGE
www.mintagevintage.com
This is the best such outlet on West Cordova, with a varied stock and witty displays. Second outlet at 1714 Commercial Drive.
N4   320 West Cordova Street   ☎ 604/MIN-TAGE
Waterfront   4, 7, 8, 10, 16, 20, 50

RICHARD KIDD
www.richardkidd.net
There is no missing this store, fronted by an enormous glass wall. It's hard to resist walking in, even if the prices are eye-watering and many of the designer clothes are more like works of art.

COMMERCIAL DRIVE
Commercial Drive runs for almost 20 blocks and lies some 2km (1.2 miles) east of Chinatown. It's a gritty area, and will be too far east for most visitors, but it is one of the city's emerging quarters and has a variety of independent stores and places to eat and drink (take a taxi or bus 20). Standout stores are Magpies (1319 Commercial Drive at Charles ☎ 604/253-6666), a superb magazine shop; Virgin Mary's (1035 Commercial Drive at Venables ☎ 604/844-7848) for vintage fashion; and Dutch Girl Chocolates (1002 Commercial Drive at Venables ☎ 604/251-3221) for confectionery.

N4   65 Water Street at Abbott   ☎ 604/677-1880
Waterfront   4, 7, 8, 10, 16, 20, 50

SPIRIT WRESTLER GALLERY
www.spiritwrestler.com
Gastown gallery devoted to art and objects from First Nations peoples worldwide, including the Haida and Maori, inspired by shamanism.
N4   47 Water Street ☎ 604/669-8813 or 1-888/669-8813   Waterfront
4, 7, 8, 10, 16, 20, 50

T & T SUPERMARKET
www.tnt-supermarket.com
Large store on the edge of Chinatown that sells a vast assortment of Chinese food and other Asian products. It's fun to browse the many fruits and vegetables and other items you will probably never have seen before.
N4   179–181 Keefer Street at Abbott   ☎ 604/899-8836   Stadium   10, 16

URBAN FARE
www.urbanfare.com
A large upscale supermarket devoted to organic fruit and vegetables, ethnic and healthy foods, and high-quality ready meals. Excellent bakery, pasta bar and other specialist counters.
M5   177 Davie Street at Pacific Boulevard
☎ 604/975-7550
Yaletown-Roundhouse
15, C23

Entertainment and Nightlife

AFTERGLOW

www.glowbalgrill.com

Small, mellow lounge attached to the Glowbal Grill (▷ 59), with candles, an intimate atmosphere and easy-listening music. Ideal for drinks whether or not you eat at the restaurant.

➕ M5 ✉ 1079 Mainland Street at Helmcken ☎ 604/602-0835 🕒 Daily 11.30am–1am 🚇 Yaletown-Roundhouse 🚌 6, 15, C23, N15

ALIBI ROOM

www.alibi.ca

One of Gastown's hippest bar-restaurants, but not so cool that it is off-putting. The lower floor lounge is where most people drink; eclectic but well-prepared food is served in the more roomy area upstairs.

➕ N4 ✉ 157 Alexander Street at Columbia ☎ 604/623-3383 🕒 Tue–Sun 5pm–midnight or later 🚇 Waterfront 🚌 4, 7, 8, 50, N20

BAR NONE

A much-frequented Yaletown bar and club, with a bare-brick-and-exposed-beam look and trendy, under-40 crowd. You can eat, drink, play pool, watch TV or use the small dance floor.

➕ M5 ✉ 1222 Hamilton Street at Davie ☎ 604/689-7000 🕒 Daily (may close Wed and for private functions) 🚇 Yaletown-Roundhouse 🚌 6, 15, C23, N23

THE CAMBIE

www.thecambie.com

A big pub that attracts local office workers, back-packers and other visitors staying at the adjoining, co-owned hostel. Has a big, bare-brick bar, but in summer most people use the roomy terrace. Low prices for food and beer.

➕ N4 ✉ 300 Cambie Street at West Cordova ☎ 604/688-9158 🕒 Daily 11am–1am or later 🚇 Waterfront 🚌 3, 4, 7, 8, 10, 16, 20, 50, N20

CAPONE'S

www.caponesrestaurant.net

House pianists and trios play live jazz early in the week while you dine on

DANCE

Vancouver is a major hub for dance. The main focus is the Scotiabank Dance Centre (✉ 677 Davie Street; www.thedancecentre.ca), whose website offers information on venues, performances and links to other sites. Festivals include the biennial Dance in Vancouver (odd years), plus the Vancouver International Dance Festival in March (☎ 604/662-7441, www.vidf.ca) and 10-day Dancing on the Edge festival of contemporary dance in July (www.dancingontheedge.org). Major companies include Ballet British Columbia (www.balletbc.com) and the Anna Wyman Dance Theatre (www.annawyman.com).

pastas or pizzas at this friendly Yaletown restaurant. Friday and Saturday attract bigger names. Arrive early or book to be near the stage.

➕ M5 ✉ 1141 Hamilton Street at Davie ☎ 604/684-7900 🕒 Daily 11.30am–late 🚇 Yaletown-Roundhouse 🚌 6, 15, C23, N23

ELIXIR

www.elixirvancouver.ca

Opus was Yaletown's first funky boutique hotel (▷ 112) and its restaurant and late bar are equally trendy. Enjoy French bistro food in the restaurant. There is also a lighter garden room and more decadent area of red wood-paneling and red banquettes. Robert de Niro and Harrison Ford have enjoyed a nightcap here in the past.

➕ M5 ✉ Opus Hotel, 350 Davie Street at Richards ☎ 604/642-0557 🕒 Mon–Sat 6.30am–2am, Sun 6.30am–midnight 🚇 Yaletown-Roundhouse 🚌 6, 15, C23, N23

FABRIC

www.fabricvancouver.com
www.clubzone.com

The name changes from time to time, but what-ever is over the door, this venue is usually at the forefront of the Gastown club scene. Great sound system, top DJs, and up-to-the-minute music.

➕ N4 ✉ 66 Water Street at Abbott ☎ 604/683-6695 🕒 Thu 9pm–2am, Fri–Sat

9pm–3am Waterfront 4, 7, 8 50, N20

FIREHALL ARTS CENTRE

www.firehallartscentre.ca
An old fire station is the setting for this 150-seat venue and leading community arts center. It hosts mostly contemporary and avant-garde music, mime, dance and other visual arts.
P4 280 East Cordova Street at Gore 604/689-0926 Main 4, 7, 8, 35, N35

GEORGE ULTRALOUNGE

www.georgelounge.com
A popular, smart Yaletown bar that attracts a young, good-looking crowd for champagne and sophisticated cocktails.
M5 1137 Hamilton Street at Helmcken 604/628-5555 Mon–Sat 5pm–2am Yaletown-Roundhouse 6, 15, C23, N23

LOTUS SOUND LOUNGE

www.lotussoundlounge.com
Moody lighting in an underground dance club that hosts themed music nights, with an emphasis on house and techno. Friday night is especially popular. The same venue has a couple of other excellent bar-clubs, Lick and Honey.
N4 Lotus Hotel, 455 Abbott Street at West Pender

604/685-7777 Wed–Sat 9pm–3am Waterfront 10, 16, 20, 50, N20, N35

SHINE

www.shinenightclub.com
The place for a fun and uncomplicated night out. Convenient Gastown location, friendly staff, fair prices, themed music nights (good DJs) and lively fellow clubbers. Saturday is the big night.
N4 364 Water Street at Richards 604/408-4321 Daily 9pm till late Waterfront 4, 6, 7, 8, 10, 16, 20, 50, N20

STEAMWORKS

www.steamworks.com
Gastown microbrewery that sells around a dozen

JAZZ FESTIVAL

Even in a city renowned for its many festivals, The International Jazz Festival (☎ 604/872-5200; www.coastaljazz.ca) stands out, a world-class jazz-and-blues event that runs for 10 days, usually from the third Friday of June. More than 800 musicians gather, including some of the biggest names in jazz (performers have included Diana Krall and the late Oscar Peterson). Some 25 venues are used—anything from nightclubs to open-air spaces on Grouse Mountain. There are free events and the festival includes a two-day Mardi Gras-style street festival in Gastown.

of its own beers. Has a different character on different levels—German beer hall in the cellar and upstairs a club-like wood-paneled area with comfortable chairs overlooking the water.
N4 375 Water Street 604/689-2739 Daily 11.30am–late Waterfront 4, 6, 7, 8, 10, 16, 20, 50, N20

VANCOUVER EAST CULTURAL CENTRE

www.vecc.bc.ca
The "Cultch," as it is known locally, is a well-regarded 350-seat venue in a former church that hosts a wide range of often challenging drama, dance, mime and music.
R5 1895 Venables Street at Victoria Drive 604/251-1363 22

YALETOWN BREWING COMPANY

www.markjamesgroup.com/yaletown
Large bar and restaurant in a converted warehouse. Most people are here to drink rather than eat the Italian and West Coast food, though Sunday is popular for pizza and one of the place's own-brewed beers. The patios are great in summer.
M5 1111 Mainland Street at Helmcken 604/681-2739 Sun–Wed 11.30am–midnight, Thu 11.30am–1am, Sat 11.30am–2am Yaletown-Roundhouse 4, 6, 7, 8, 10, 16, 20, 50

Restaurants

BLUE WATER CAFÉ ($$$)

www.bluewatercafe.net
First choice in Yaletown for excellent fish and seafood. Sleek dining room of exposed brick and beams, open kitchen and "raw bar" for top-quality sushi. Amiable staff and unstuffy atmosphere.
➕ M5 ✉ 1095 Hamilton Street at Helmcken ☎ 604/688-8078 ⏰ Daily 5pm–midnight (bar to 1am) 🚇 Yaletown-Roundhouse 🚌 6, 15

CHAMBAR ($$)

www.chambar.com
Belgian restaurant with a cozy dining room, offering classics such as *moules-frites* and more exotic dishes (such as braised lamb with honey and cinnamon) and smaller-portion *petits-plats*. Belgian beer.
➕ M5 ✉ 562 Beatty Street at Dunsmuir ☎ 604/879-7119 ⏰ Daily 6pm–midnight 🚇 Waterfront 🚌 10, 16, 20

CIOPPINO'S ($$$)

www.cioppinosyaletown.com
Attractive Yaletown restaurant, with a tasteful interior of polished cherry wood. Prices may be high, but the place is relaxed and you'll enjoy some of the city's best Italian-based food.
➕ M5 ✉ 1133 Hamilton Street at Helmcken ☎ 604/688-7466 ⏰ Mon–Sat 5–10.30 🚇 Yaletown-Roundhouse 🚌 15

COAST ($$$)

www.coastrestaurant.ca
Near neighbor and competitor of the Blue Water Café, serving similarly good fish and seafood, but in a more contemporary setting. Fish comes from BC and "coasts" around the world.
➕ M5 ✉ 1257 Hamilton Street at Drake ☎ 604/685-5010 ⏰ Daily 4.30pm–midnight 🚇 Yaletown-Roundhouse 🚌 6, 15

DRINK LOCAL

Canadian wine used to be a joke but standards have improved markedly—so take advantage and drink local. Some wine comes from Vancouver Island (look for Wild Goose and Starling Lane), but most is made in the Okanagan region, home to more than 100 wineries. Vincor, Andrew Peller and Mission Hill are the main producers, but look for Inniskillen, Sumac Ridge, Jackson-Triggs, Gray Monk, Blue Mountain and Lakebreeze.

C RESTAURANT ($$$)

www.crestaurant.com
This waterfront restaurant opened in 1997, and its reputation for the city's best fish and seafood (often with an Asian twist) has dimmed slightly. However, the food is still imaginative and the dining experience memorable, especially if you manage to book a table on the terrace.
➕ L5 ✉ 1600 Howe Street at Beach Avenue ☎ 604/681-1164 ⏰ Daily 5–10 🚇 Yaletown-Roundhouse 🚌 G4, 7, 10 ⛴ Ferry from Granville Island

FLOATA SEAFOOD ($–$$)

www.floata.com
Floata accommodates more than 1,000 diners, making it Canada's largest Chinese restaurant. Dim sum at lunch is good; dishes in the evening are more adventurous and more expensive. Set menus are good options.
➕ N5 ✉ 180 Keefer Street at Québec, 3rd floor of mall ☎ 604/602-0368 ⏰ Daily 7.30am–10.30pm 🚇 Main 🚌 3

GLOWBAL GRILL ($$)

www.glowbalgrill.com
Classic Asian-West Coast fusion cooking in a hip but unpretentious Yaletown restaurant that is also a laid-back lounge and late-night bar. Good-value lunch specials, but the cool dining room is best suited to the evening.

🚇 M5 ✉ 1079 Mainland Street at Helmcken ☎ 604/602-0835 🕐 Daily 11.30am–1am 🚊 Yaletown-Roundhouse 🚌 6, 15, C23

HON'S WUN-TUN HOUSE ($)

Hon's has been around forever—its recipe of rock-bottom prices, low-tech dining room and vast menu of Chinese staples (over 330 items) having been so successful, it now has outlets beyond its original Chinatown home.

🚇 P5 ✉ 268 Keefer Street at Gore ☎ 604/688-0871 🕐 Daily 11–11 🚊 Main 🚌 3

INCENDIO ($)

www.incendio.ca

A laid-back and funky pizzeria (also pastas and inventive salads), with plenty of room and bold decor, including splashy works of art.

🚇 N4 ✉ 103 Columbia Street at Alexander ☎ 604/688-8694 🕐 Mon–Thu 11.30–3, 5–11, Fri 5–11, Sat 4.30–11, Sun 4.30–10 🚊 Waterfront 🚌 4, 6, 7, 8, 10, 16, 20, 50

PHNOM PENH ($)

Vancouver's best Vietnamese and Cambodian cooking, as the frequent lines of locals waiting to be seated testify. Lots of wonderful dishes, especially the soups with fish, chicken or pork; crisp chicken salad with mint and spicy garlic crab.

🚇 P5 ✉ 244 East Georgia Street at Main ☎ 604/682-5777 🕐 Daily 10–10 🚊 Main 🚌 3, 8, 19

PINK PEARL ($)

www.pinkpearl.com

Pink Pearl is an institution, in business more than 25 years, and though in a dingy part of the city (take a cab), it is bustling, authentic and full of Chinese diners. Strong on dim sum and seafood.

🚇 Q4 ✉ 1132 East Hastings Street at Glen Drive ☎ 604/253-4316 🕐 Mon–Thu, Sun 9am–10pm, Fri–Sat 9am–11pm 🚌 3

RODNEY'S OYSTER BAR ($$)

A top spot for oysters (plus chowder and other seafood) in Yaletown—

DIM SUM

Most Chinese restaurants offer dim sum—meaning "small heart" or "to touch the heart"—an assortment of small, inexpensive dishes. There are over 2,000 varieties, but most restaurants will offer around 150, almost always at lunch (10–2), and on Sundays in particular. Jasmine or other tea is usually brought to your table after you arrive, followed by carts filled with plates or bamboo baskets of food. Point to what you want and your choices will be marked on a bill that generally stays on your table until you finish.

"The lemon, the oyster and your lips are all that is required" is the claim here.

🚇 M5 ✉ 1228 Hamilton Street at Davie ☎ 604/609-0080 🕐 Mon–Sat 11am–midnight, Sun 3–9.30 🚊 Yaletown-Roundhouse 🚌 6, 15

SOCIAL AT LE MAGASIN ($$)

www.socialatlemagasin.com

Trendy restaurant in a 1911 Gastown heritage building, with oyster bar downstairs and striking tin-ceiling restaurant and bar upstairs (plus back-room butcher's and deli for vast sandwiches and more to take out or eat in the bar). Superb steaks and a tempting brunch menu.

🚇 N4 ✉ 332 Water Street at Cambie ☎ 604/669-4488 🕐 Restaurant Mon–Fri 11–3.30, 5–11, Sat–Sun 10–4, 5–11. Deli Mon–Sat 11–7, Sun noon–6 🚊 Waterfront 🚌 4, 7, 50

WATER STREET CAFÉ ($$)

Opposite Gastown's Steam Clock, this café-restaurant is a pretty and relaxed place for lunch or dinner (book for an outside table in summer). The short menu features mostly contemporary Italian dishes.

🚇 N4 ✉ 300 Water Street ☎ 604/689-2832 🕐 Daily 10am–10.30pm or later 🚊 Waterfront 🚌 4, 6, 7, 8, 10, 16, 20, 50

The mainly residential South Vancouver covers a large area beyond Downtown, but its highlights—Granville Island, the museums of Vanier Park, and the laid-back Kitsilano neighborhood—are all within easy reach of the city center.

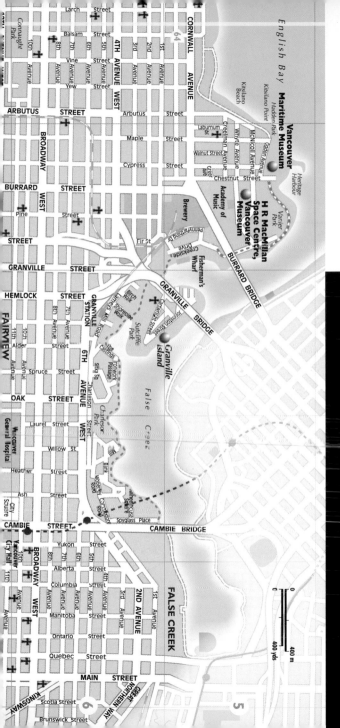

English Bay

CORNWALL AVENUE

Larch Street
Balsam Street
Vine Street
Yew

Connaught Park

10th
8th Avenue
7th Avenue
6th Avenue
5th Avenue
4TH AVENUE WEST
3rd Avenue
2nd Avenue
1st Avenue

64

Kitsilano Point
Kitsilano Beach

Maritime Museum

Hadden Park

McNicoll Avenue

Creelman Avenue

Ogden Avenue

Whyte Avenue

Vancouver

Heritage Harbour

ARBUTUS STREET

BROADWAY

Arbutus Street

Maple Street

Cypress Street

Laburnum St
Walnut Street

Creek Ave

Chestnut Street

BURRARD WEST STREET

Pine Street

STREET

Brewery

Academy of Music

Vanier Park

H R MacMillan Space Centre, Vancouver Museum

Creekside Drive

Penny Farthing Dr

GRANVILLE STREET

First St

Fisherman's Wharf

BURRARD BRIDGE

HEMLOCK STREET

GRANVILLE STATION

8th Avenue
7th Avenue

GRANVILLE STREET

Birch Walk
Cartwright Street
Mill Statue Road
Lameys Mill Road
Shoreline Walk

GRANVILLE BRIDGE

Johnston Street

FAIRVIEW

11th Avenue
10th Avenue
Alder Street

6TH AVENUE WEST

Spruce Street

Ironwork Passage
Sitka Sq
The Castings
Charleson Park
Harrison Park

Sutcliffe Park

Granville Island

OAK STREET

Laurel Street

Willow St

False Creek

Vancouver General Hospital

Heather Street

Ash Street

Bimi
McBride Court
Moberly Road
Wheelhouse Court
Spyglass Place

City Square

CAMBIE STREET

Vancouver City Hall

BROADWAY

8th
7th
6th
5th
4th Avenue
3rd Avenue
2ND AVENUE
1st Avenue

Yukon Street
Alberta Street
Columbia Street
Manitoba Street
Ontario Street
Quebec Street

CAMBIE BRIDGE

FALSE CREEK

MAIN STREET

KINGSWAY

Scotia Street
Brunswick Street

GREAT NORTHERN WAY

6

5

0   400 m
0   400 yds

Granville Island

Granville Island is one of Vancouver's most popular attractions, thanks to its wonderful medley of shops, galleries, museums and a superlative food market.

Transformation Originally swampland, the island was drained in 1916 and became one of the city's main industrial sites, only to fall into decline in the 1960s, prompted by fires and the exodus of most of the businesses. Thereafter it became a vermin-infested dumping ground, recovery only taking hold in 1972, when the government financed a $25-million regeneration scheme. The result was inspired, mixing residential, commercial and light-industrial projects, lending the area a gritty sense of vitality and purpose it might otherwise lack.

Market and museums Most people come here for the superlative market (very busy on weekends)—there can be few better places to buy food in North America—and the galleries, specialist stores and artisans' workshops. Be sure to explore, notably at the southern end of Johnson and Cartwright streets—children will love the Kids' Market on the latter, as well as the restored streetcar, or Downtown Historic Railway (DHR), that runs to Science World (▷ 48). You can also tour the small Granville Island Brewery (GIB), or visit the island's three linked museums, devoted to model trains, model ships and sport fishing. There are a handful of restaurants for formal dining, and the Backstage Lounge (▷ 75) is one of several good places for a drink, perhaps before a show at the adjoining Arts Club (▷ 75).

THE BASICS

www.granvilleisland.com

➕ L5

🍴 Many cafés, restaurants and food stalls

🚌 50

⛴ Aquabus and False Creek services

♿ Good

ℹ 1661 Duranleau Street, tel 604/666-5784

Food Market

☎ 604/666-6477

🕐 Daily 9–7

Kids' Market

✉ 1496 Cartwright Street

☎ 604/689-0820

🕐 Daily 10–6

Downtown Historic Railway

🚃 Corner of 2nd Avenue and Old Bridge Street

☎ 604/665-3903

🕐 Every 30 minutes Sat–Sun and public hols mid-May to mid-Oct 12–5

💷 Inexpensive

Granville Island Brewery

✉ 1441 Cartwright Street

☎ 604/687-2739

🕐 3 tours daily: times vary

💷 Moderate

Museums

✉ 1502 Duranleau

☎ 604/683-1939

🕐 Tue–Sun 10–5.30

💷 Moderate (combined ticket to all three museums)

H.R. MacMillan Space Centre

TOP 25

Discover the wonders of space at this popular attraction

THE BASICS

www.hrmacmillanspace centre.com

✚ K5

✉ 1100 Chestnut Street at Whyte Avenue

☎ 604/738-7827

🕐 Daily 10–5 (closed Mon Sep–end Jun)

🍽 Café

🚌 2, 22

⛴ Aquabus and False Creek services to Vanier Park

♿ Excellent

💷 Expensive (▷ below)

HIGHLIGHTS

● Interactive displays
● Star shows
● Laser shows

TIP

● A combined $30 Explorepass is available for entry to the Space Centre, Vancouver Museum and Maritime Museum from the visitor center (▷ 122) and the sights.

Vancouver's high-tech Space Centre explores every facet of space and space travel, and offers spectacular star and other shows in its planetarium.

Heavens above The Space Centre is devoted to all aspects of space and the science of space and, like the similar Science World, is packed with modern hands-on interactive displays that are immensely popular with children. As a result, the center is often busy with large school parties and other tour groups, so aim to arrive early or late to avoid the rush. Among other things, the exhibits allow you to battle an alien, plan a voyage to Mars, guide a lunar probe and design a spaceship. Especially popular is the Virtual Voyages Simulator, which gives you some idea of what it is like to be aboard a spacecraft, or to collide with a comet. Also popular are the film presentations in the Ground Station Canada theater, which run roughly hourly for 20 minutes from mid-morning.

Star shows The center also incorporates the MacMillan Planetarium, which offers several shows daily on the stars (usually afternoons), but also loud, brash laser shows (usually at weekends only, additional admission), often accompanied by rock music. The laser shows are very popular, so arrive in good time or book tickets ahead. Set apart from the center is the Gordon Southam Observatory, a small, domed building with a telescope that can be used for public star-gazing at weekends, weather allowing. Entry is free, but check with the Space Centre for current opening times.

Museum of Anthropology

Vancouver's finest museum is away from the center, but its superbly displayed totem poles and other aboriginal arts and artifacts make it worth the journey.

World-class The superb concrete-and-glass building housing the museum was designed in 1976 by Arthur Erickson, one of North America's leading architects, its bright and spacious interior inspired by the post-and-beam houses of the region's aboriginal peoples. The museum is part of the University of British Columbia (UBC) campus, 30 minutes by bus or taxi from the city. Wooden entrance doors, carved by aboriginal sculptors, usher you onto the Ramp, lined with sculptures rescued from sites across the Pacific Northwest region. Eventually you reach the spectacular Great Hall, a majestic setting for the finest collection of totem poles and other monumental aboriginal art.

Hidden treasures Vast windows in the Great Hall look out to the ocean over the grounds, which contain a reconstructed village typical of the Haida people. Off the Great Hall are some Visible Storage Galleries—drawers and cases with some of the 35,000 artifacts from Canadian and other aboriginal cultures. These are like a lucky dip, each one revealing—among other items—sublime pieces of jewelry, fabrics, or fine stone and other carvings. Some of the loveliest works of art are in the Anniversary Galley, opened in 1999 to mark the museum's 50th anniversary. Don't miss *The Raven and the First Men*, a vast wooden sculpture carved by aboriginal artist Bill Reid.

THE BASICS

www.moa.ubc.ca
+ B6
✉ 6393 NW Marine Drive
☎ 604/822-3825 or 604/822-5087
🕐 Mid-May to mid-Oct daily 10–5 (plus Tue 5–9); rest of year Wed–Sun 11–5 (plus Tue 5–9)
🍽 Café
🚌 4, 17, 44 to UBC, then 10-minute walk
♿ Excellent
💲 Moderate. By donation Tue 5–9
❓ The museum is undergoing renovation; phone 604/822-5950 for information

HIGHLIGHTS

● The Great Hall
● Museum grounds

TIPS

● The museum is not easy to find. Consult maps or ask students for directions.
● Don't miss the gardens on the UBC campus.

Vancouver Maritime Museum

TOP 25

A maritime heritage is celebrated with displays and original artifacts

THE BASICS

www.vancouvermaritime
museum.com

K5

✉ 1905 Ogden Avenue at
Chestnut Street

☎ 604/257-8300

🕐 May–end Aug daily
10–5; Sep–end Apr Tue–Sat
10–5, Sun 12–5

🚌 2, 22

⛴ Aquabus and False
Creek services from
Granville Island

♿ Good

💲 Moderate

HIGHLIGHTS

● Heritage Harbour
● *St. Roch*

TIPS

● The museum's Discovery
Centre has interactive
displays aimed at children.
● Combine a visit here with
a visit to the Space Centre
(▷ 66) and the Vancouver
Museum (▷ 69).

Vancouver's port and maritime traditions are explored using models, original ships and other artifacts in this quaint and old-fashioned museum.

Traditional The best approach to this museum—one of a trio of sights in Vanier Park—is by ferry from Granville Island. The boats dock at a small jetty known as Heritage Harbour, which often has a collection of small historic boats. This sets the marine tone for the museum itself, a short walk away, which lacks the hands-on displays of many contemporary museums, but whose more traditional, old-fashioned approach is well-suited to the wide range of maritime exhibits on display.

Eagle aerie En route to the museum, don't miss the Mungo Martin totem, carved from a 600-year-old red cedar, a replica of the totem presented to the Queen in 1958, to mark British Columbia's centenary. Bald eagles use the pole as a perch.

Star of the sea Among the museum's collection are original charts from the ships of George Vancouver, the British seafarer who claimed the area that would become Vancouver for the British Crown in 1792. There are also model ships and evocative period photographs of 19th-century Vancouver. The Discovery Centre is popular with children, who, among other things, can dress up as pirates. The museum's star turn, though, is the *St. Roch*, a beautiful 1928 Royal Canadian Mountain schooner and the first vessel to navigate the Northwest Passage in a single season.

Vancouver Museum

The Vancouver Museum (left) has a diverse range of exhibits (middle and right)

The Vancouver Museum explores the city's history with the help of temporary exhibitions and a vast array of aboriginal and more recent artifacts.

Historical record Vancouver's main city museum is not in the same league as Victoria's Royal BC Museum (▷ 98), but it still offers a good overview of the city's origins, along with the story of the lower mainland of British Columbia. It's especially good on Vancouver's 19th- and early 20th-century development, though for a full exploration of the area's fascinating aboriginal history, be sure to combine a visit here with one to the Museum of Anthropology (▷ 67).

Haida to hippy The museum dates from 1968, its conical shape an allusion to the cedar-bark hats worn by the Haida people who once inhabited the area. In front of the building stands a strange fountain that alludes to the mysterious crab-like creature of aboriginal legend that guards the entrance to the city's harbor. Vancouver's 8,000-year-old aboriginal past is further explored inside the museum, with tools, clothes and other items, including a whaling canoe. Thereafter, the displays move on to a roughly chronological and self-contained survey of such things as the exploits of early explorers; exhibits related to the lumber industry; and a life-size section of an immigrant ship. Fun displays devoted to the 20th century include exhibits illustrating 1950s pop culture and the hippy movement that took hold in the city, especially in the nearby Kitsilano district (▷ 70).

THE BASICS

www.vanmuseum.bc.ca
✚ K5
✉ 1100 Chestnut Street at Whyte Avenue
☎ 604/736-4431
🕐 Jul–end Sep Mon–Wed, Fri–Sun 10–5, Thu 5–9pm; Oct–end Jun Tue–Wed, Fri–Sun 10–5, Thu 5–9pm
🍴 Café
🚌 2, 22
🚢 Aquabus and False Creek services to Vanier Park
♿ Excellent
💰 Expensive (▷ Tip, 66)

HIGHLIGHTS

● Whaling canoe
● Re-created immigrant vessel
● Forestry displays

TIPS

● An hour or two will be sufficient for most visits.
● Allow time to visit the adjoining H.R. MacMillan Space Centre (▷ 66).

More to See

KITSILANO

Kitsilano (known as Kits more commonly) is the mainly residential district, roughly between West 16th Avenue and the waterfront and Alma and Burrard streets. In the 1960s it was famous as the heart of the Vancouver counterculture, beloved of the city's hippies. Today, its leafy streets are among the city's most desirable, but some of the old ethos survives, though in a more affluent guise—lots of great cafés and restaurants, wonderful shops, a laid-back air and a thriving arts, cultural and nightlife scene. Most of the cafés and shops are on and around West 4th Avenue and West Broadway, though in summer the focus is Kitsilano Beach, a fine stretch of sand backed by an attractive park.

✚ J6 🚌 2, 7, 22, 32, 44, 84

★ NITOBE MEMORIAL GARDEN

www.nitobe.org

Turn right out of the Museum of Anthropology (▷ 67) and a five-minute walk brings you to this small Japanese garden, begun over 40 years ago to honor Dr. Inazo Nitobe (1862–1933), a scholar and champion of pan-Pacific relations. Considered one of the most authentic Japanese gardens outside Japan, it is a beautiful and tranquil retreat of sloping paths, streams, fountains and precisely placed floral elements.

✚ B6 ✉ 1895 Lower Mall, near Gate 4, Memorial Road ☎ 604/822-6038 🕐 Mid-Mar to mid-Oct daily 10–6; mid-Oct to mid-Mar Mon–Fri 10–2.30 🚌 4, 17, 44 then 10-minute walk ♿ Very good 🖐 Inexpensive. Mid-Oct to mid-Mar free. Joint ticket with UBC Botanical Garden, moderate

QUEEN ELIZABETH PARK

Vancouver's third-largest park wraps around southern Vancouver's highest point (167m/548ft), the rump of an old volcano that offers sweeping views north to the ranks of Downtown skyscrapers and the mountains beyond. At the top of the hill are the Quarry Gardens, rock gardens dotted with ponds,

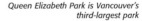

Sweeping Kitsilano Beach, perfect in fine weather

Queen Elizabeth Park is Vancouver's third-largest park

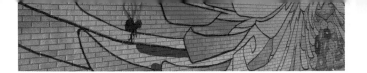

fountains and waterfalls, while on the eastern slopes are examples of every tree native to Canada. The natural highlights are in the Bloedel Floral Conservatory, with desert, subtropical and rain-forest habitats and climates. Inside are 500 species of plants and 50 species of birds.

➕ M9–N9 ✉ West 33rd Avenue at Cambie ☎ 604/257-8584 ⏲ Daily 24 hours 🍴 Seasons in the Park (▷ 78) 🚇 King Edward (Canada Line due to open Nov 2009) 🚌 15

SOMA

SoMa means "South of Main" and refers to a rather down-at-heel but increasingly chic enclave of Vancouver's eastern suburbs, a district that used to be known simply as Mount Pleasant. It embraces Main Street from around 6th Avenue to 29th Avenue, with the best tracts of bohemian stores, trendy cafés and quirky boutiques situated between 6th and 10th and 20th and 29th avenues. It's still rough round the edges, and perhaps too

far east for casual visitors, but this is one of the city's coolest emerging neighborhoods. At 33rd Avenue you could head west to see Queen Elizabeth Park or push south to 49th Avenue to explore the rambling four-block Punjabi Market and "Little India" ethnic district.

➕ N7 🚌 3

UBC BOTANICAL GARDEN

www.ubcbotanicalgarden.org

This garden is almost directly opposite the Nitobe Memorial Garden (▷ 70), but is larger and older. Established in 1916, it was Canada's first botanical garden, and has more than 10,000 species of plants, trees and shrubs, divided into eight thematic gardens. Highlights are the BC Native Garden, the winter garden and medieval apothecary garden. The garden also has Canada's largest collection of rhododendrons and the Botanical Garden Shop for books, garden implements and shrubs and plants.

➕ B7 ✉ 6804 SW Marine Drive at West 16th Avenue ☎ 604/822-9666 ⏲ Mid-Mar

SoMa is a vibrant and trendy district (below and right)

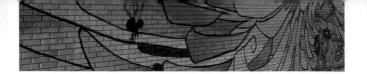

to mid-Oct daily 10–6; mid-Oct to mid-Mar 10–4 🚌 4, 17, 44 then 15-minute walk ♿ Very good ⚑ Moderate. Mid-Oct to mid-Mar free. Joint ticket with Nitobe Memorial Garden moderate

VANDUSEN BOTANICAL GARDEN

www.vandusengarden.org

Horticulture magazine rates this 22ha (54-acre) green oasis as one of the world's top 10 botanical gardens, though the UBC Botanical Garden (▷ 71) has its champions among Vancouverites. A golf course until 1960, it opened as a garden in 1975, and is made up of 40 specialized mini-gardens. Highlights include the Elizabethan Hedge Maze, containing over 1,000 pyramid cedars; the Rose Garden; Lake Garden; Rhododendron Walk; and Korean Pavilion—the last given over to Asiatic plants. There are usually daily guided tours (free) and regular cart tours for seniors or those with disabilities. The garden is easily seen in conjunction with Queen Elizabeth Park (▷ 70–71).

🞣 L9 ✉ 5251 Oak Street at West 33rd Avenue and West 37th Avenue ☎ 604/878-9274 🕐 Mar, Oct daily 10–5; Apr 10–6; May 10–8; Jun–end Aug daily 10–9; Sep daily 10–7; Nov–end Feb daily 10–4 🍴 Café on site 🚉 King Edward (Canada Line due to open Nov 2009) 🚌 17 to Oak Street ♿ Very good ⚑ Moderate

WRECK BEACH

www.wreckbeach.org

Vancouver's most famous beach is 1km (0.6 miles) south of the Nitobe Memorial Garden (▷ 70), and is accessed from SW Marine Drive near Gate 6, at the foot of University Boulevard. The beach's fame—or infamy—stems from the fact that for years it was an enclave beloved only of nudists, hippies and other harmless renegades. These days it has become more crowded and commercialized, with food-sellers, hawkers and people offering massages, body-painting and the like. However, it is a lovely beach, bordered by the ocean on one side and trees on its three other flanks.

🞣 B7 ✉ UBC Campus, SW Marine Drive

Admire the assorted, ornate planting of the well-tended Botanical Garden

Shopping

LES AMIS DU FROMAGE

www.buycheese.com
A cheese shop extraordinaire, with anything up to 500 different varieties from across the globe. Knowledgeable staff will help you choose from the enormous selection. Also has a large range of crackers, preserves and other accompaniments.
➕ K6 ✉ 1752 West 2nd Avenue at Burrard ☎ 604/732-4218 🚌 2, 22

BARBARA-JO'S BOOKS TO COOKS

www.bookstocooks.com
Excellent specialist bookshop in Kitsilano, with over 2,500 cookery, food and wine books, plus fiction and other literary works with a gastronomic theme. Also offers occasional cooking classes, talks and demonstrations.
➕ K6 ✉ 1740 West 2nd Avenue at Burrard ☎ 604/688-6755 🚌 2, 22, 44

COMOR OUTDOOR

www.comorsports.com
One of the key shops in the chain of outdoor, surf and other activity stores that cluster in pockets of south Vancouver. A major stockist of ski and winter sports clothing and equipment, as well as hiking, surf, beach and other wear. It also rents equipment and will deliver to most major central hotels.
➕ K6 ✉ 1980 Burrard Street at 4th Avenue ☎ 604/736-7547 🚌 5, 22, 44

EQUINOX GALLERY

www.equinoxgallery.com
Art sales flourish in Vancouver, with many galleries based in south Vancouver, especially on Granville Street around West 7th Avenue. Equinox is one of the longest-established, and even if the prices are too high, it is worth dropping by to admire the work of big-name national and international artists.
➕ K6 ✉ 2321 Granville Street at West 7th Avenue ☎ 604/736-2405 🚌 10, 16, 17

GRANVILLE ISLAND

Granville Island (▷ 65) is an exhilarating shopping experience. Many of its craft stores and galleries are in the Net Loft building. Also see the Craftshouse Gallery (1386 Cartwright Street; www.cabc.net), run by the Crafts Association of British Columbia, and the Gallery of BC Ceramics (1359 Cartwright Street). Standout food concessions in the market include Dussa's for ham and cheese; Oyama (www.oyamasausage.ca) for sausages and other meat products; Granville Island Tea Company (www.granvilletea.com), with over 150 types of tea; and the Stock Market for homemade soups, stocks and other products to eat in or take out.

GRAVITY POPE

www.gravitypope.com
This big Kitsilano store is the city's best shoe shop, offering every form of footwear, from the lowliest flip-flop to showy designer creations.
➕ J6 ✉ 2205 West 4th Avenue at Yew ☎ 604/731-7673 🚌 4, 7, 44, 84

KAPLAN'S

www.kaplans.ca
Kaplan's is a little piece of old Vancouver, a wonderfully authentic Jewish delicatessen that dates from the 1940s but has been given a light makeover (new black and white tiles and green vinyl banquettes). It also functions as a restaurant, and among the 265 menu items are some fantastic sandwiches and numerous kosher options. You'll find the shop just to the southwest of Queen Elizabeth Park. There is also a Downtown outlet at 1059 Alberni Street.
➕ L9 ✉ 5775 Oak Street at 41st Avenue ☎ 604/251-3711 🍴 Delicatessen Mon–Wed 9–6, Thu–Sun 9–8. Restaurant Mon–Wed 11–6, Thu–Fri 11–8, Sat–Sun 10–6

KIDSBOOKS

www.kidsbooks.ca
Canada's largest kids' bookstore is an obvious first choice in Kitsilano if you're traveling with children who love reading, or have run out of vacation books. There are also lots of toys and games and

⊞

other activities to divert kids, plus special events and regular readings by authors.
✚ H6 ✉ 3083 West Broadway at Balaclava ☎ 604/738-5335 🚌 2, 9, 17, 22

MARK JAMES
www.markjamesclothing.com
A major menswear store selling Paul Smith, Armani and other designer names. It's also a casual, jeans and sportswear shop.
✚ H6 ✉ 2941 West Broadway at Bayswater ☎ 604/734-2381 🚌 9, 17

MAYFAIR NEWS
Offers an extraordinary selection of national and international newspapers and magazines, including more than 120 national daily newspapers in 10 languages.
✚ K6 ✉ 1535 West Broadway at Granville ☎ 604/738-8951 🚌 9, 10, 16, 17, 98

MEINHARDT FINE FOODS
www.meinhardt.com
Narrow aisles and deli-counters packed with gourmet foods and ingredients, including breads, cheeses and meats, plus an adjoining patisserie and café for lunch and take-out food.
✚ K7 ✉ 3002 Granville Street at West 14th Avenue ☎ 604/732-4405 🚌 10, 98

MOUNTAIN EQUIPMENT CO-OP
www.mec.ca
One of Canada's oldest and largest outdoor equipment stores, and a city institution, this block-long megastore really is a co-operative, so you need to pay a small fee to join. However, this cost is easily recouped from the savings you'll make when buying from its staggering assortment of outdoor goods.
✚ N6 ✉ 130 West Broadway at Manitoba ☎ 604/872-7858 🚌 9, 99

OUTDOOR ITEMS
It could just be that there is nowhere better in the world than Vancouver to buy outdoor equipment. Mountain Equipment Co-Op (▷ above) spawned several competing stores in the surrounding blocks on West Broadway around Cambie and Columbia streets, notably Valhalla (222 West Broadway; www.vpo.ca) and AJ Brooks (147 West Broadway; www.ajbrooks.com).

Farther west, a similar thing happened with skate, surf, ski, diving and snowboard stores, which cluster near the junction of West 4th Avenue and Burrard Street. The key store here is Pacific Boarder (1793 West 4th Ave at Burrard Street; www.pacificboarder.com).

PURDY'S
www.purdys.com
Purdy's has outlets across western Canada, and several stores in Vancouver, including in the Pacific Centre Mall (▷ 34). It sells a sublime selection of chocolates and confectionery.
✚ K6 ✉ 2705 Granville Street at West 11th Avenue ☎ 604/732-2705 🕒 Mon–Sat 10–6, Sun 12–5

SHAUGHNESSY ANTIQUE GALLERY
Offers a wide range of Victoriana, but specializes in pieces from the 1950s, '60s and '70s.
✚ K7 ✉ 3080 Granville Street at West 16th Avenue ☎ 604/739-8413 🚌 10, 98

SIGGE'S
www.sigges.com
Sigge's is largely devoted to winter sports, and cross-country and other types of skiing in particular. You can also pick up snowshoes and other equipment.
✚ J6 ✉ 2077 West 4th Avenue at Arbutus ☎ 604/731-8818 🕒 Closed May–end Aug 🚌 4, 7

ZULU RECORDS
www.zulurecords.com
Music-lovers, and fans of vinyl, secondhand and rarities will spend hours at this Kitsilano record store, which also stocks new and used CDs.
✚ K6 ✉ 1972 West 4th Avenue at Maple ☎ 604/738 3232 🚌 4, 7

THE ARTS CLUB

www.artsclub.com

A mainstay of Vancouver's theatrical scene, the Arts Club began as a group of actors in the 1960s, moving to Granville Island in 1979. It has three venues, including the Granville Island Stage on its home turf. The dozen or so productions a year run the gamut, but can be of varying quality.
➕ L5 ✉ 1585 Johnston Street, Granville Island ☎ Box office 604/687-1644 ⏰ Box office Mon–Sat 10am–showtime, Sun noon–5 🚌 50

BACKSTAGE LOUNGE

www.thebackstagelounge.com

A popular and long-established bar and live-music venue on Granville Island that forms part of the Arts Club (▷ above). Has DJ-led dance nights and live jazz, blues and R&D some nights. It's an easygoing spot for a drink looking over the water, a light meal or a nightcap—there's a selection of more than 50 whiskies.
➕ L5 ✉ 1585 Johnston Street, Granville Island ☎ 604/687-1354 ⏰ Mon–Sat noon–2am, Sun noon–midnight 🚌 50

BIN 942

www.bin941.com

Sister establishment to the successful Bin 941 (▷ 38), and with a similar approach—small, cozy and convivial, with small-portion 'tapatizers' to eat, plus a good

selection of beers and wines by the glass.
➕ K6 ✉ 1521 West Broadway at Granville ☎ 604/734-9421 ⏰ Daily 5pm–2am 🚌 9, 17

BRIDGES

www.bridgesrestaurant.com

A reliable and popular choice for food or a drink on Granville Island, with a restaurant upstairs in the hard-to-miss waterfront building and a bistro and pub downstairs. Most people, though, opt for the large outdoor terrace.
➕ L5 ✉ 1696 Duranleau Street ☎ 604/687-4400 ⏰ Restaurant daily 5.30–10, bistro daily 11am–midnight, pub Mon–Sat 11am–1am, Sun 11am–midnight 🚌 5

BROLLYWOOD

In the last decade, low costs and spectacular scenery—plus an urban environment that can double for US or Asian cities—have turned Vancouver into one of North America's largest film and TV production centers. The city has been named Hollywood North, or, more unkindly, Brollywood—Hollywood with rain. The X-Files was one of the first high-profile TV shows, and First Blood with Sylvester Stallone and The Accused with Jodie Foster are just two of the big-name movies made here. Visit www.bcfilmcommission.com for details of films currently being shot locally.

CELLAR RESTAURANT & JAZZ CLUB

www.cellarjazz.com

This small, 70-person venue, with red walls, black booths and low tables, is the best place to hear jazz in Kitsilano. Spotlights local talent, but also attracts national and international touring acts.
➕ G6 ✉ 3611 West Broadway at Dunbar ☎ 604/738-1959 ⏰ Daily 6pm–midnight. Live music generally six nights per week, with sets at 8 and 10.30 🚌 9

CHIVANA

www.chivana.com

Hip hideaway that attracts the odd Hollywood actor working in the city. Brown walls, a big fireplace and elegantly "distressed" decor, with a distinctive 12m (40ft) bar and a covered patio.
➕ J6 ✉ 2340 West 4th Avenue at Vine ☎ 604/733-0330 ⏰ Daily 5pm–late 🚌 4, 7

DOCKSIDE BREWING COMPANY

www.docksidebrewing.com

A stylish and attractive bar that has been serving beer from its own micro-brewery for more than 30 years. In winter, settle down by the fire, while in summer there's a fine patio with views of the waterfront and the mountains beyond. Try the Cartwright Pale Ale and fruity Jamaican Lager.
➕ M5 ✉ Granville Island Hotel, 1253 Johnston Street

☎ 604/685-7070 ◐ Daily 7am–10.30pm, Fri–Sat open to 11.30pm; kitchen closes 10pm daily 🚍 50

EARLY MUSIC VANCOUVER

www.earlymusic.bc.ca
www.pacificbaroqueorchestra.com

Promotes medieval, baroque and other early music, usually played on original instruments, with concerts at various venues around the city. Has an active role in the Early Music Festival in August.

✚ K6 ✉ 1254 West 7th Avenue ☎ 604/732-1610

HELL'S KITCHEN

www.hells-kitchen.ca
Popular with Kitsilano's young and trendy, who come here primarily to drink (though the food is good, too). A dark, moody color scheme (hence the name) adds to a boozy and bustling vibe.

✚ J6 ✉ 2041 West 4th Avenue at Arbutus ☎ 604/736-4355 ◐ Mon–Fri 11.30am to 1am or later, Sat–Sun 10am–2am 🚍 4

THE NAAM

www.thenaam.com
A Kitsilano institution, founded in 1968 during the area's hippy heyday, The Naam still has a funky, alternative feel. The health and vegetarian food can be worthy and, although the service is famously hit-and-miss, it's still a popular

spot, especially at weekends. There's also live music some nights, prices are low and it's open 24 hours.

✚ H6 ✉ 2724 West 4th Avenue at MacDonald ☎ 604/738-7151 ◐ 24 hours daily 🚍 2, 4, 7, 22

ROSSINI'S KITS BEACH

www.rossinisjazz.com
Not a place to come to straight off the beach, despite the name, but rather a stylish bar and restaurant that appeals to 30- and 40-something locals. Offers good, mainstream live jazz most nights.

✚ J5 ✉ 1525 Yew Street at Cornwall ☎ 604/737-8080 ◐ Daily 11am–2am 🚍 2, 22

CINEMA

The rise of DVDs and home entertainment has killed off countless movie houses in Vancouver. However, the city still has some thriving art-house, repertory and independent cinemas. One of the best in Downtown is Pacific Cinémathèque (1131 Howe Street at Helmcken; www.cinematheque.bc.ca), with a schedule that changes daily, while in Kitsilano the big draw is the much-loved 1950 Ridge Theatre (3131 Arbutus Street at West 16th Avenue; www.festival cinemas.ca), which presents a mix of foreign, art-house and Hollywood movies.

UBC SCHOOL OF MUSIC

www.chancentre.com
www.music.ubc.ca
The university music school performs around eight major and many smaller concerts during the year, many of them free. The 1,400-seat Chan Centre for the Performing Arts on the campus is a premier performance space.

✚ B6 ✉ School, UBC Recital Hall, Gate 4, 6391 Memorial Road. Chan Centre, 6265 Crescent Road ☎ School 604/822-3113. Chan Centre 604/822-9197 🚍 4, 17, 44

VANCOUVER BACH CHOIR

www.vancouverbachchoir.com
The city's leading, non-professional choir is 150-strong and performs three to five major works a year at the Orpheum Theatre.
☎ 604/921-8012

VANCOUVER CHAMBER CHOIR

www.vancouverchamberchoir.com
Vancouver's top professional choir was founded in 1971 and offers a wide range of popular concerts—anything from jazz and gospel to avant-garde and a cappella. The season runs from late September to May, with performances at around a dozen different venues.
☎ 604/738-6822

Restaurants

Prices are approximate,
based on a 3-course
meal for one person.
$$$ over $40
$$ $20–$40
$ under $20

ARBUTUS ($)

A delightful neighbor-
hood café inside a
heritage building largely
unchanged since its days
as a 1920s grocer's store.
Wonderful soups, pies
and paninis.
➕ J6 ✉ 2200 Arbutus Street
at West 6th Avenue ☎ 604/
736-5644 ⏲ Mon–Fri 6–6,
Sat–Sun 8–6 🚌 4, 7

BISHOP'S ($$$)

www.bishopsonline.com
Founder John Bishop
more or less invented the
fusion of French, Asian
and Italian that domi-
nates the cuisine of most
Vancouver restaurants.
This venue, opened in
1985, is still one of the
best and you'll need to
book ahead.
➕ J6 ✉ 2183 West 4th
Street at Yew ☎ 604/738-
2025 ⏲ Daily 5–11 🚌 4, 7

BISTROT BISTRO ($$)

www.bistrotbistro.com
Warm and welcoming
European-style bistro that
offers good-value and
high-quality French coun-
try cooking. The colorful
interior is cozy in winter
and airy in summer,
when the large picture
windows are opened.
➕ K6 ✉ 1961 West 4th
Avenue at Cypress ☎ 604/
732-0004 ⏲ Tue–Thu
5–11pm, Fri–Sat 5–midnight,
Sun 5–10pm. Closed Mon
🚌 4, 7

GALLEY PATIO & GRILL ($)

www.thegalley.ca
An inexpensive and
unpretentious place for
a drink and simple fish-
and-chip supper while
enjoying the sunset and
waterfront views from
the patio - but arrive
early for an outdoor
perch, as reservations
are not taken.
➕ F5 ✉ Jericho Sailing
Centre, 1300 Discovery Street
☎ 604/222-1331 ⏲ Spring
and fall daily 11am–sunset;
summer 9am–10pm; winter
Sat–Sun 11am–sunset 🚌 4

FOOD WITH A VIEW

The best places for food
with a view are: Dockside
Brewing Company (▷ 75);
Fish House at Stanley Park
(▷ 39); Galley Patio & Grill
(▷ 77); Go Fish (▷ 77);
Lift Bar & Grill (▷ 40);
Prospect Point Café (▷ 40);
Sailor Hagar's (▷ 90);
Salmon House on the Hill
(▷ 90); Seasons in the Park
(▷ 78); Sequoia Grill at the
Teahouse (▷ 40); and the
Vancouver Lookout (▷ 49).
Panoramic patios are in
demand, so always try
to book ahead for an
appropriate table.

GASTROPOD ($$–$$$)

www.gastropod.ca
Gastropod won numer-
ous awards for Best
Newcomer when it
opened in 2007, though
its minimalist dining room
and adventurous cutting-
edge cuisine, which owes
much to the "scientific
gastronomy" of Britain's
Heston Blumenthal, will
not be to all tastes.
➕ K6 ✉ 1938 West
4th Avenue at Cypress
☎ 604/730-5579 ⏲ Daily
5.30–10.30 🚌 4, 7

GO FISH ($)

Many locals believe this
shack on the seawall
between Granville Island
and Vanier Park serves
the city's best fish and
chips. Fish is bought from
the boats that dock near-
by: When it's finished for
the day, the shack shuts
up shop. There are daily
specials, plus soups, salads, slaw and oyster, tuna
or salmon sandwiches.
➕ K5 ✉ 1505 West 1st
Avenue at Creekside Drive
☎ 604/730-5040 ⏲ Tue–Fri
11.30–6, Sat–Sun 12–6 🚌 50

LUMIÈRE ($$$)

www.lumiere.ca
Canadian celebrity chef
Rob Feenie, who helped
put Lumière on the map,
left in 2007, but the
mostly contemporary
French food here
continues to dazzle.
➕ J6 ✉ 2551 West
Broadway at Trafalgar ☎ 604/
739-8185 ⏲ Tue–Sun
5.30pm–11pm 🚌 9

PANE FROM HEAVEN ($)

A convenient place for Fairtrade coffee, a snack or light lunch after seeing the Vancouver Museum, Space Centre and Maritime Museum in nearby Vanier Park. The panini and homemade soups are really good.

➕ K5–6 ✉ 1688 Cypress Street at West 1st Avenue ☎ 604/736-5555 🕒 Mon–Sat 7–6 🚌 2, 22

ROCKY MOUNTAIN FLATBREAD CO ($$)

www.rockymountainflatbread.ca
Gourmet thin-crust pizzas made from wholesome (often organic) locally sourced ingredients. Popular with families and convenient for Vanier Park and its museums.

➕ K6 ✉ 1876 West 1st Avenue at Cypress ☎ 604/730-0321 🕒 Daily 11.30–9.30 🚌 2, 22

SANDBAR ($$)

www.vancouverdine.com/sandbar
Sandbar offers a convenient and informal escape from the crowds of Granville Island, and is especially good for families with children. It's large and airy, and spread over several levels, with a vaguely nautical decorative theme. The mostly fish and seafood is reliable but unexciting. Locals use the Sandbar more as a bar than a restaurant, especially on Friday and Saturday.

➕ L5 ✉ 1535 Johnston Street, Granville Island ☎ 604/669-9030 🕒 Daily 11.30–10 or later 🚌 50

SEASONS IN THE PARK ($$–$$$)

www.vancouverdine.com
The perfect fine-dining lunch spot in Queen Elizabeth Park, with sophisticated dishes that are as good as the romantic setting and views. Booking ahead is essential.

➕ M9 ✉ Queen Elizabeth Park, West 33rd Avenue at Cambie ☎ 1-800/632-9422 🕒 Daily 11.30–2.30, 5.30–9.30 🚇 King Edward (Canada Line due to open Nov 2009) 🚌 50

WEST COAST AND FUSION

Time and again in Vancouver you'll see cuisine described as fusion, West Coast, Pacific Northwest, Pacific Rim–even Californian. All mean a mixture of predominantly Italian-influenced dishes (with some French thrown in) that fuse some of the ideas and ingredients of other ethnic cuisines, in particular those of Asia. Latterly, this style of cooking has also emphasized the use of seasonal and locally sourced organic ingredients. John Bishop (Bishop's, ▷ 77) was the pioneer of an approach that is now almost ubiquitous in Vancouver.

SOPHIE'S COSMIC CAFÉ ($)

www.sophiescosmiccafe.com
A kitsch 1950s-style diner and Kits fixture since 1988; hugely popular, especially weekday lunch-times and at weekends (the brunch is super). Admire the memorabilia while tucking into the celebrated breakfasts. The mussels, milkshakes and burgers are excellent.

➕ J6 ✉ 2095 West 4th Avenue at Arbutus ☎ 604/732-6810 🕒 Daily 8am–9.30pm 🚌 4, 7

VIJ'S ($$)

www.vijs.ca
Vij's wins awards for the city's best Indian cooking year after year. To see why, you'll probably have to wait in line, as reservations are not taken, or head next door to Rangoli, a café with take-out food from Vij's.

➕ K6–7 ✉ 1480 West 11th Avenue at Granville ☎ 604/736-6664 🕒 Daily 5.30–10pm 🚌 10

WEST ($$$)

www.westrestaurant.com
Regularly vies with Bishop's (▷ 77) for the title of Vancouver's best restaurant, with which it shares an approach of West Coast fusion cooking, seasonal menus and, where possible, local organic ingredients.

➕ K7 ✉ 2881 Granville Street at West 13th Avenue ☎ 604/738-8938 🕒 Daily 5.30–11pm 🚌 10

A separate part of the city, across the waters of the Burrard Inlet, North Vancouver has several mountain and forest parks that offer an easily accessible taste of Canada's great outdoors.

Grouse
Mountain

Lynn
Headwaters
Regional
Park

NORTH VANCOUVER

29TH STREET EAST

LYNN VALLEY ROAD

Mount Seymour
Provincial Park

Lynn Canyon
Park

18

CITY OF
NORTH
VANCOUVER

DRIVE

19

21

22

MOUNT SEYMOUR PARKWAY

Lonsdale
Quay

DOLLARTON HIGHWAY

23

SeaBus

Vancouver
Harbour

d

e

Capilano River

HIGHLIGHTS

● Cleveland Dam
● Salmon Hatchery
● Capilano Suspension
Bridge
● River trails
● Ambleside Park

TIPS

● Combine the Capilano
River sights with Grouse
Mountain (▷ 84).
● Access sights and trails by
bus or taxi along Capilano
Road–Nancy Greene Way
parallel to the river.

The Capilano River boasts a range of attractions, from the trails and canyons of the river itself to a fascinating salmon hatchery and dizzying suspension bridge.

Walks and views The Capilano River tumbles 32km (20 miles) from the slopes of the North Shore mountains to the Pacific just west of the Lions Gate Bridge. Much of its lower reaches are protected by the Capilano River Regional Park, which is laced with 26km (16 miles) of well-tended trails along or near the river. Within the park, just 1km (0.6 miles) south of the Grouse Mountain cable-car station (▷ 84), is the Cleveland Dam, source of 40 percent of Vancouver's water. Walk across the dam for great views, and consult the trail board by the parking lot for details of other easy walks locally: The best is the Giant Fir Trail to

Clockwise from left: The winding Capilano River; test your nerve on the Capilano Suspension Bridge; Capilano River Regional Park is ideal for outdoor enthusiasts; the Treetops Adventure; the entrance to Capilano Suspension Bridge; the Capilano Salmon Hatchery

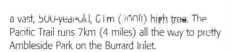

THE BASICS

www.britishcolumbia.com/ RIVERS

🚌 c2

🚢 SeaBus then 236 from Lonsdale Quay

Salmon Hatchery

www.pac.dfo-mpo.gc.ca

✉ 4500 Capilano Park Road

☎ 604/666-1790

🕐 Daily Jun–end Aug 8–8 May, Sep 8–7; Apr, Oct 9–4.45; Nov–end Mar 8–4

♿ Good

🎟 Free

Suspension Bridge

✉ 3725 Capilano Road

☎ 604/985-7474

🕐 Daily Apr 9–6.30; May, Jun, Sep 8.30–8; Jul–end Aug 8.30am–9pm; Oct 9–6; Nov–end Mar 9–5

🍴 Café

♿ Good

🎟 Expensive

a vast, 500-year-old, 61m (200ft) high tree. The Pacific Trail runs 7km (4 miles) all the way to pretty Ambleside Park on the Burrard Inlet.

Salmon hatchery Trails also lead south to the Capilano Salmon Hatchery, built to encourage salmon stocks after the dam compromised the spawning grounds. It's a fascinating place, with the chance to watch salmon struggling upstream to spawn and to observe fish at various stages of their development. More lovely trails run alongside the river to the south, but most visitors head to the privately owned Capilano Suspension Bridge. Although busy and commercialized, the 137m (150-yard) bridge offers tremendous views of the river gorge 70m (230ft) below. In 2005, the Treetops Adventure was added, a series of small suspension bridges high above the forest floor.

Grouse Mountain

TOP 25

Grouse Mountain cable car (left); sculpture on Grind Trail (middle); superb views (right)

THE BASICS

www.grousemountain.com
✛ d1
✉ 6400 Nancy Greene Way
☎ 604/980-9311/980-0661
🕔 Skyride daily every 15 minutes 9am–10pm
🍴 Altitudes Bistro ($) and Observatory Restaurant ($$$) in Alpine Centre. Starbucks at Skyride base station
🚆 SeaBus to Lonsdale Quay, then bus 236
♿ Good
💰 Expensive

HIGHLIGHTS

● Cable-car ride
● The views
● Lumberjack shows

TIPS

● Arrive early to avoid lines.
● Combine a visit with Capilano River (▷ 82–83).
● Evening dinner reservations at the Alpine Centre's Observatory Restaurant include the price of Skyride.

North America's largest cable cars run up Grouse Mountain, a natural vantage point where you can enjoy superlative views of Vancouver and its surroundings.

Up and away Grouse Mountain (1,250m/ 4,100ft) is just a short bus ride from Lonsdale Quay, and offers a taste of the wild scenery on Vancouver's doorstep. Arrive early to avoid a wait in line and climb aboard the Skyride, vast 100-person cable cars (known as gondolas in Canada) that in eight panoramic minutes climb to the Alpine Station, at 1,128m (3,700ft). Here you'll find various dining options, a souvenir store and the Theatre in the Sky, where your Skyride ticket is valid for short film presentations about the mountain and British Columbia. You can also walk up Grouse Mountain on the aptly named Grouse Grind Trail, a popular but strenuous and rather monotonous hike.

Activities at altitude Beyond the Alpine Station, walkways fan out across meadows, where in summer (May–end September) you can see free shows and demonstrations. These include guided walks (ask at the small information kiosk just beyond the Alpine Centre), lumberjack shows (usually three daily), a wolf enclosure, falconry displays and an enclosure with two orphaned grizzly bears. Bikes can also be rented and helicopter tours arranged. The mountain is also popular in winter, with free sleigh rides, skating and around 25 ski and snowboarding runs. The mountain has more than 1.1 million visitors a year.

Escape to the peaceful beauty of Lynn Canyon Park

Lynn Canyon Park

Lynn Canyon is a protected pocket of beautiful river and forest scenery, a taste of wilderness on the mountain slopes a few minutes above Lonsdale Quay.

Crowd-free country While most people flock to Grouse Mountain and the Capilano Suspension Bridge to the west, the Lynn Canyon Park remains relatively unvisited, making it perfect for those who want a genuine taste of Vancouver's outdoors without straying far from Downtown. It is also far less crowded and commercialized than Capilano, though here, too, there is a suspension bridge; a touch smaller, but free to cross and with fine views of the creek. The Ecology Centre, just inside the park entrance, acts as an information and interpretive center, with maps and pamphlets plus videos and displays on the area's flora and fauna.

Easy hiking Come in your boots or walking shoes to tackle several easy and well-marked trails of up to 90 minutes through forest, along gorges and past cliffs and waterfalls. The most popular are the 15-minute Thirty-Foot Pool Trail and the Twin Falls Trail, a 40-minute loop from the suspension bridge. Note that much longer and more ambitious hikes are possible. As you walk, you pass through so-called "second-growth" forest, that is, forest that has regenerated after its original trees have been felled. Most of the timber here had been cut by the beginning of the 20th century, but the size of the existing forest suggests the fecundity of the temperate rain forest and the advantages of 150cm (60 inches) of rain a year.

THE BASICS

⊞ d2–e2
◷ Daily 7am–dusk
🍴 Lynn Canyon Café ($)
🚌 SeaBus to Lonsdale Quay then bus 228 or 229 to Peters Road (20 min)
♿ Poor
🖐 Free

Ecology Centre
www.dnv.org/ecology
✉ 3663 Park Road, off Peters Road
☎ 604/990-3755
◷ Jun–end Sep daily 10–5, Oct–end May 12–4
🖐 Donation; free guided walks Jul–end Aug

HIGHLIGHTS

● Ecology Centre
● Suspension Bridge
● Forest trails

TIP

● The park is 20 minutes from Lonsdale Quay by bus, then a 5- to 10-minute walk from the nearest bus stop.

Mount Seymour Provincial Park

TOP
25

Dawn at Mount Seymour Provincial Park (left); views of Mount Baker (right)

THE BASICS

www.env.gov.bc.ca/bcparks

☩ e1–e2

✉ 1700 Mount Seymour Road

☎ 604/986-2261

◔ Daily 24 hours

🚌 SeaBus to Lonsdale Quay, then bus 239 to Phibbs Exchange and 215 to Mount Seymour-Indian River

♿ Poor

👖 Free

❓ For park maps go to: www.env.gov.bc.ca/bcparks

HIGHLIGHTS

● Mount Seymour Road viewpoints
● Forest habitats
● Hiking trails

TIPS

● A full day is needed to do the park justice and make a trip worthwhile.

● Access is possible by public transportation, but a car is preferable.

Mount Seymour Provincial Park is the wildest of the easily accessible scenery close to Vancouver, and a popular outdoor playground in summer and winter.

Taste of the wild Mount Seymour is the largest and most easterly of the parks close to Vancouver's Downtown core, but it's an hour's drive or bus ride away. It is best for those staying longer in the city who are keen to see scenery that most closely resembles British Columbia's rugged interior. You stand a good chance of seeing coyotes and deer close to Mount Seymour Road, the 13km (8-mile) approach, while black bears, cougars and bobcats are not unknown in the park. Two forest habitats co-mingle here, the coastal western hemlocks and mountain hemlock zones, creating rich biodiversity, and some vast "old-growth" Douglas firs and western red cedars.

Top trails Mount Seymour Road is dotted with trailheads for several hikes, as well as some superb viewpoints, notably Deep Cover Lookout. Most people wait until the parking lot at the top of the road before donning their walking boots. The easiest hike here is the Goldie Lake Loop, a 30-minute, 2km (1.2-mile) stroll through some of the oldest forest. About the same length, but with a 180m/590ft elevation gain, is the Mystery Lake Trail. The park's most popular walk is the Mount Seymour Trail (4km/2.5-mile round-trip, 450m/1,476ft elevation), a two-hour hike with a stiff climb, rewarded with lovely views from the summit of Mount Seymour (1,455m/4,740ft).

Downtown Vancouver (left); Lonsdale Quay (middle); the scenic SeaBus (right)

TOP 25

SeaBus

NORTH VANCOUVER ★ **TOP 25**

On the face of it, the SeaBus is simply a ferry that links Downtown with North Vancouver, but for visitors it also provides one of the city's most scenic rides.

Best views Many of the world's most spectacular cities have scenic ferry rides and Vancouver is no exception. For a couple of dollars you can board the SeaBus and enjoy glorious panoramas not only of the Downtown skyline, but also of the city's great port.

The practicalities The SeaBus service uses two 400-seat catamarans that ply a route across the Burrard Inlet between Waterfront Station (▷ 52) on the Downtown peninsula (between Canada Place and Gastown) and Lonsdale Quay (▷ 88) in North Vancouver. The journey takes 12 minutes and services run every 15 or 30 minutes. Even if you only wish to see Lonsdale Quay and then return, without exploring North Vancouver, the ride is worthwhile for the journey alone

The ride At first the mountains of the North Shore dominate the views, but mid-way across you come close to tugs, container ships, cruise liners and the other bustling life of a port that includes 233km (144 miles) of waterfront and 276km (171 miles) of navigable water. As you approach the North Shore, you'll see the vast piles of sulphur, timber and other cargo handled in the port. Looking back across the water, you now also see the magnificent skyline of Downtown, etched with skyscrapers and framed by Stanley Park.

THE BASICS

www.translink.bc.ca

➕ c2

✉ Waterfront Station, 601 West Cordova Street at foot of Granville Street

☎ 604/953-3333

🕐 Mon–Sat 6.15am–12.45am, Sun 8.15am–11.15pm

🍽 Cafés at Lonsdale Quay and Waterfront Station

Ⓦ Waterfront

🚌 6, 44, 50 and services to Granville Street

♿ Excellent

💲 Inexpensive

❓ Bikes may be taken on board SeaBus

HIGHLIGHTS

● Close-up views of the port
● The Downtown skyline

TIPS

● Sit at the front, back or side to enjoy the best views.
● The SeaBus ride is a two-zone transit journey (▷ 118, 119).

More to See

CYPRESS PROVINCIAL PARK

www.cypressmountain.ca

You will need a car to visit the most westerly and most popular of the big parks protecting the mountains of the North Shore. Access is via the Cypress Parkway (which offers fine views), 15km (9 miles) off exit 8 on Hwy 1-99 at Cypress Bowl Road. Many of the park's trails start from the parking lot at the top of the Cypress Parkway, notably the easy Yew Lake (2km/1.2-mile round-trip; 45 min) and Black Mountain Loop (2.5km/1.5-mile, 45 min, 100m/328ft elevation gain). The area is a prime winter sports destination.

🔢 b1 ✉ Cypress Bowl Road ☎ Park 604/924-2200; winter sports 604/926-5612 🕐 Daily 24 hours 🖐 Free

LIGHTHOUSE PARK

Lighthouse Park is a small protected semi-wild coastal enclave on the westerly tip of the North Shore, 10km (6 miles) west of the Lions Gate Bridge. It has the advantage of being easily accessible by public transportation. Sea-smoothed granite boulders and low bluffs run along the shoreline, backed by huge stands of Douglas firs and other virgin forest, some of it over 1,500 years old. Trails include two easy paths to the 1912 Atkinson Point lighthouse that gives the park its name (5km/3-mile round-trip).

🔢 a2 ✉ Beacon Lane and Marine Drive ☎ 604/925-7200 🕐 Dawn to dusk 🚌 250 from Lonsdale Quay 🖐 Free

LONSDALE QUAY

www.lonsdalequay.com

Lonsdale Quay is several things: the North Vancouver terminus for SeaBus services (▷ 87) from the city's Downtown peninsula; a major bus terminus for services throughout North and West Vancouver; and home to a superb market that combines food and other stalls with around 80 specialist gourmet and other stores. Buy food or picnic provisions from the many concessions, stalls and cafés and sit on the waterfront terrace to admire the views across the Burrard Inlet.

🔢 d2 ⛴ SeaBus from Waterfront Station **Lonsdale Quay Market** ✉ 123 Carrie Cates Court ☎ 604/985-6261 🕐 Mon–Sat 9.30–6.30 (later opening Fri); dining options remain open later 🖐 Free

The cityscape of Vancouver is spectacular after dark

For a taste of the wilderness visit Lighthouse Park (right and opposite)

Entertainment and Nightlife

PRESENTATION HOUSE THEATRE
www.phtheatre.org
This former schoolhouse has been turned into a venue that hosts mostly contemporary theater and performance art.
🔱 d2 ✉ 333 Chesterfield Avenue ☎ 604/606-990 3474 🚢 SeaBus Lonsdale Quay

THE RAVEN
www.theravenpub.com
An excellent and relaxed pub offering several imported beers and over 20 microbrewery

choices, plus malts and pub food.
🔱 f2 ✉ 1052 Deep Cove Road ☎ 604/929-3834
🕙 Daily 11am–midnight
🚍 212 🚢 SeaBus Lonsdale Quay

RUSTY GULL
www.rustygullpub.com
The food and occasional live music at this neighborhood pub are good, and the view from the patio is great.
🔱 d2 ✉ 175 East 1st Street at Lonsdale Avenue ☎ 604/988-5585
🕙 Fri–Sat 10am–1am,

Sun–Thu 11am–midnight
🚢 SeaBus Lonsdale Quay

SAILOR HAGAR'S
www.bestbeerbc.com
An unpretentious pub and microbrewery three blocks west of Lonsdale Quay, with its own beers, plus a wide range of other ales. Outdoor patio, live jazz (usually Sunday nights) and pub food.
🔱 d2 ✉ 86 Semisch Avenue at West 1st ☎ 604/984-3087 🕙 Sun–Thu 11am–midnight, Fri–Sat 11am–1am 🚢 SeaBus Lonsdale Quay

Restaurants

PRICES

Prices are approximate, based on a 3-course meal for one person.
$$$ over $40
$$ $20–$40
$ under $20

GUSTO DI QUATTRO ($)
www.quattrorestaurants.com
Accomplished and good-value Italian cooking in a smart but laid-back family restaurant near the waterfront.
🔱 b2 ✉ 1 Lonsdale Avenue ☎ 604/924-4444
🕙 Dinner daily from 5pm, lunch Mon–Fri 🚢 SeaBus to Lonsdale Quay

OBSERVATORY ($$$)
www.grousemountain.com
The food is expensive, but you are paying for the extraordinary view below you from close to the summit of Grouse Mountain (▷ 84).
🔱 d1 ✉ Grouse Mountain ☎ 604/980-9311 🕙 Daily 5–10pm 🚍 236 from Lonsdale Quay

SALMON HOUSE ON THE HILL ($$–$$$)
www.salmonhouse.com
The name of this restaurant says it all: salmon (and other fish and seafood) form the basis of the seasonal menu and the hillside setting offers a captivating panorama.

🔱 b1 ✉ 2229 Folkstone Way, off Hwy 1-99 1km (0.6 miles) east of junction of Hwy 1-99 and Cypress Bowl Road ☎ 604/926-3212
🕙 Mon–Sat 11.30am–2pm, 5pm–11pm, Sun 11am–2pm, 5pm–11pm 🚍 251

TOMAHAWK ($)
www.tomahawkrestaurant.com
The long-standing Tomahawk is North Vancouver's first choice for warming comfort food (especially weekend brunch), such as chicken pies and meatloaf.
🔱 c2 ✉ 1550 Philip Avenue near Marine Drive ☎ 604/988-2612 🕙 Sun–Thu 8am–9pm, Fri–Sat 8am–10pm 🚍 240

Many visitors to Vancouver also travel to Victoria, British Columbia's intimate provincial capital across the water on Vancouver Island. Outdoor enthusiasts should also visit Whistler, one of North America's finest resorts.

Sights	**94–102**	Top 25		**TOP 25**
Walk	**103**	Butchart Gardens ▷ **94**		
		Gulf Islands ▷ **96**		
Entertainment		Victoria ▷ **98**		
and Nightlife	**104**	Whale-watching ▷ **100**		
		Whistler ▷ **101**		
Restaurants	**105–106**			

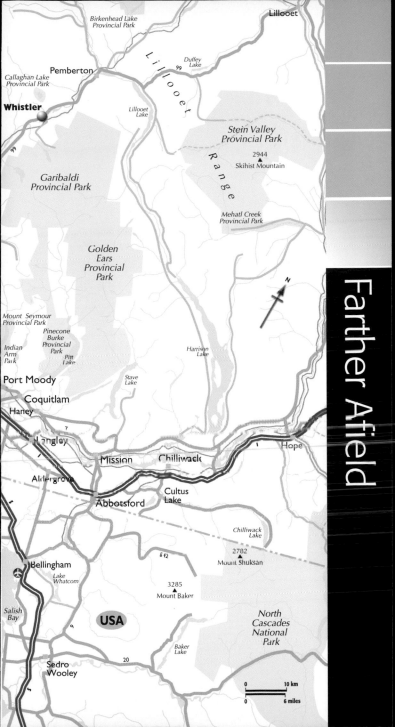

Butchart Gardens

TOP
25

Popular and much publicized, these extensive gardens north of Victoria are a must for anyone with even the slightest horticultural interest.

Transformation Much of Vancouver Island is lush and fertile, ideal for gardeners. In contrast, the Butchart Gardens had inauspicious origins, begun in 1904 by Jenny Butchart to landscape one of the quarries belonging to her husband, R.P. Butchart, a mine-owner and the pioneer of Portland cement in Canada and the US. Today, they extend across 20ha (50 acres), with over a million plants and shrubs and 700 different floral and arboreal species. Among the various specialist areas are rose, Japanese and Italianate gardens. Bear in mind that the gardens are hugely popular, especially with tour-bus groups. Much space is

Now a National Historic Site of Canada, the splendid Butchart Gardens feature a vast array of flowers and plants, lush ornamental gardens and decorative sculptures and fountains throughout the grounds

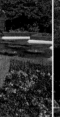

also given over to the gardens' commercial and visitor facilities—the parking area, dining options and large gift shop.

Flowers and fireworks In the summer (mid-June to mid-September) the gardens are illuminated during their extended opening times, creating a magical effect. Most summer Saturday evenings also include firework displays, and there are often classical music recitals. If you've come to Victoria without your own transportation, it's easy to get to the gardens, either on public transportation or on one of the regular shuttles that run from May to October from the main bus terminal, centrally located at 700 Douglas Street. Note that the gardens attract over half a million visitors a year, so it pays to arrive early in the morning, or slightly out of season, to see them at their best.

THE BASICS

www.butchartgardens.com

➕ Off map to south

🔳 800 Benvenuto Gardens, Brentwood Bay, 23km (14 miles) north of Victoria

☎ 250/652 4422 or 1-866/652-4422

🕐 Mid-Jun to end Aug daily 9am–10pm; first 2 weeks of Sep and Dec 9–9; rest of the year 9am–sunset

🍴 Café and restaurant on site

🚌 75

♿ Excellent

💲 Expensive (reductions in low season)

❓ Tickets can be purchased online

Gulf Islands

The enchanting scenery of the Gulf Islands

THE BASICS

www.saltspringtourism.com
www.galianoisland.com
www. mayneisland
chamber.ca
www.penderislandchamber.
com
www.bcferries.com
🚫 Off map to south
✉ Saltspring visitor center,
121 Lower Ganges Road
☎ 250/537-5252 or 250/
537-4223
🍴 La Berengerie, House
Piccolo, Hummingbird Pub,
Treehouse Café (▷ 105)
🚢 BC Ferries services to all
islands from Tsawwassen
❓ Accommodations infor-
mation www.hellobc.com
or www.gulfislands
reservations.com

HIGHLIGHTS

● Scenic ferry crossing
● Unspoiled coastal scenery

TIP

● The islands are popular, so
book accommodations early.

The narrow straits between Vancouver and Vancouver Island are scattered with a bucolic archipelago of beautiful islands.

Distant promise All most people see of the Gulf Islands is a view from afar: either from above, as they fly by seaplane between Vancouver and Victoria, or at closer hand from a BC Ferries ship from Tsawwassen (the ferry terminal south of Vancouver), as it navigates between several of the islands on its beautiful, 90-minute sailing to Swartz Bay on Vancouver Island, north of Victoria. Even this brief glimpse is enough to whet the appetite, for even from a distance you can see that these islands appear impossibly idyllic: small, peaceful and pastoral, and fringed with coves, bays and secret beaches. Make the effort to visit, and the distant promise is confirmed.

Island pleasures If you have the time, all the islands are served by regular ferries from Tsawwassen and Swartz Bay, but the most con-venient for a short visit are Salt Spring and Galiano and, to a lesser extent, Pender and Mayne. All have accommodations options, often small guest-houses, but beds are limited, so be sure to book well in advance in summer. All are also more or less the same, in that the pleasures they offer are a languid, easy-going way of life, browsing galleries (the island life has attracted many artists), visiting a neighborhood café, buying organic produce from roadside stalls, idling on a beach, gentle hiking, or renting a bicycle to amble around the tranquil lanes. Sailing and fishing are also big activities.

Victoria

HIGHLIGHTS

- Inner Harbour
- Royal BC Museum
- Old Town
- Whale-watching (▷ 100)

TIPS

- Victoria's highlights can be seen in a day if you take a seaplane (▷ 119) to and from Vancouver.
- Victoria is 35 minutes by seaplane (▷ 119) and 3 hours 30 minutes by bus-ferry from Vancouver.

Victoria is one of North America's most enticing small cities, easily visited from Vancouver, and worth an overnight stay to do justice to its many sights.

Capital city British Columbia's provincial capital is a delightful place, more town than city, with a lovely waterfront, flower-hung streets, gardens, a small old quarter full of interesting shops, cafés and restaurants, and a medley of sights of which many a larger city would be proud. At its heart is the Inner Harbour, a lovely waterfront esplanade, dominated by the Parliament Buildings (guided tours) and the landmark Empress Hotel, famed for its afternoon teas. Alongside the former is the Royal BC Museum (RBCM), Victoria's highlight, a majestic museum devoted to all aspects of British Columbia past and present.

THE BASICS

www.tourismvictoria.com

➕ Off map to south

🍴 Cafés and restaurants (▷ 105–106)

♿ Good

❓ Seaplane (▷ 119) or combined bus-ferry options are available to get from Vancouver to Victoria

ℹ 812 Wharf Street, tel 250/953-2033 (accommodations 1-800/663-3883); Jun–end Aug daily 8.30–8.30; Sep–end May 9–5

Royal BC Museum

www.royalbcmuseum.bc.ca

✉ 675 Belleville Street

☎ 250/356-7226

🕐 Daily 9–5

💲 Moderate

Historical legacy In the museum's shadow is Helmcken House, one of several historic buildings, a legacy of Victoria's early role as the main white settlement in Western Canada. The city began as a Hudson's Bay Company trading post, but in the 1850s—well before the growth of Vancouver—became a staging post for gold prospectors heading for the mainland. Point Ellice House and Craigdarroch Castle are other key historic buildings open to the public. The Maritime Museum is also worth a look, part of the delightful old town (Victoria walk, ▷ 103) behind the Inner Harbour, where, among other things, you should also explore the small Chinatown and the shops of Market Square. Victoria is known as the "Garden City," its finest green space being Beacon Hill Park, south of the Royal BC Museum, full of shady corners and with some dazzling ocean views.

Whale-watching

Whale-watching trips are available in the waters around Victoria

THE BASICS

www.5starwhales.com
www.princeofwhales.com
www.seacoastexpeditions.com

✚ Off map to south

✉ Five Star Whale Watching, 706 Douglas Street; Prince of Whales, 812 Wharf Street; Seacoast Expeditions, Coast Victoria Harbourside Hotel, 146 Kingston Street

☎ Five Star Whale Watching 250/388-7223 or 1-800/634-9617; Prince of Whales 1-250/383-4884 or 1-888/383-4884; Seacoast Expeditions 250/383-2254 or 1-800/386-1525

🕓 Most companies offer between three and five 3- or 4-hour trips daily May–Sep, one or two daily Oct–Apr

♿ Poor on Zodiacs

💰 Expensive

TIPS

● Victoria's visitor center carries details of all major whale-watching companies.
● Pack a sunhat, suncream and a waterproof jacket.

Resident and migrating orcas, minke and gray whales love the waters around Victoria, making the city one of North America's main whale-watching centers.

Why the whales? The waters around Vancouver Island lie on the 8,000km (4,970-mile) migration route of some 20,000 Pacific gray whales, which pass through the region in April and May (and back again from October to December) en route from their breeding and calving grounds in Baja, Mexico, to their summer feeding areas in the Bering and Chukchi seas off Siberia. Around 50 or so stay in the area throughout the summer, where they are joined by 30 or so small, transient pods of orca (killer whales). There are also three large pods of orcas resident in local waters. During trips, you also stand an excellent chance of seeing harbor and Dall's porpoises, harbor or elephant seals and California or stellar sea lions.

Choosing a trip Numerous whale-watching companies have sprung up in Victoria, and most have sophisticated tracking equipment that mean sightings can often be guaranteed. However, bad weather, or no whales, or too-distant whales, often mean tours are canceled, so be prepared for that. When choosing trips, consider how long companies have been operating and, just as importantly, whether you wish to take a trip on a Zodiac (a small, fast, inflatable craft) or a slower, covered boat with toilets and other facilities. Zodiacs are not suitable for pregnant women, small children or those with back problems.

The slopes of Whistler (left); Whistler Bike Park (middle); a cable-car ride (right)

Whistler

Fantastic winter sports have put this world-class resort on the map, but a wealth of tempting summer activities makes it popular year-round.

Winter wonderland Whistler was already one of the world's major recreational resorts before Vancouver was awarded the 2010 Winter Olympics, with Whistler as its main focus. The Games have brought even more attention to this superb winter and summer resort, 125km (77 miles) north of Vancouver. Winter visitors have the choice of two mountains, Whistler and Blackcomb, with some of North America's longest, highest and most varied runs (for all abilities), as well as boarding, sledging, snow-shoeing, dog-sled tours, snowmobiling and other activities. Cross-country skiing is also available.

Summer first Figures suggest that more visitors now come to Whistler in summer than winter, drawn by the beautiful scenery, the hiking and, above all, the emergence of Whistler as North America's premier mountain-biking center. You can easily rent bikes to potter on the roads around Whistler Village (as well as specialist equipment). Cable cars run up the mountains and walkers can access lots of easy but exhilarating high-level trails without having to labor up the lower slopes. Golf is also popular (there are four courses: www.golf-bc.com), as are fishing, jet-boating and rafting, plus a host of other activities. Visitor centers and the Whistler Activity Centre carry all the information you need to choose, book or pursue an activity.

THE BASICS

www.tourismwhistler.com

✚ Off map to north

ℹ 4010 Whistler Way, Whistler Village Square. Chamber of Commerce, 4230 Gateway Drive, Whistler Village

☎ Visitor information 604/932-3928 or 1-888/869-2777. Whistler Activity Centre 604/938-2769 or 1-877/991-9988

🚌 Perimeter (www.perimeterbus.com) and Greyhound (www.greyhound.ca) services from Vancouver airport, Vancouver bus terminal and selected hotels

❓ Numerous outlets offer bikes and other outdoor equipment for rent, summer and winter

TIPS

● Book accommodations in advance, summer or winter.
● Whistler Village is the best base, summer or winter, for easy access to cable cars.

More to See

BOWEN ISLAND
www.bowenisland.org
Bowen Island is 19km (12 miles)
west of Vancouver, 20 minutes
by ferry from the Horseshoe Bay
terminal. It has pretty walks along
the waterfront at Snug Bay, a small
village and ferry dock. Visit the café,
restaurants and the many galleries.
Alternatively, rent a bike or hike a
trail, notably the 4km (2.5-mile) loop
at Killarney Lake or Gardner Trail
(10km/6 miles) to the island's highest point (719m/2,359ft).
➕ Off map to west ℹ️ 432 Cardena Road,
tel 604/947-9024; May–early Sep daily 10–3;
rest of year Tue–Sat 10–3

SQUAMISH
www.tourismsquamish.com
Squamish is a scrappy former log-
ging town 64km (40 miles) from
Vancouver, just off Hwy 99, or Sea to
Sky Highway, to Whistler. It is now a
major center for climbing, windsurfing
and mountain-biking. Casual visitors
could head for the BC Museum of
Mining, 11km (7 miles) south on

Hwy 99, at a vast former copper
mine, and waterfall at Shannon Falls
Provincial Park. Brackendale, north
on Hwy 99, hosts around 2,000 bald
eagles in winter.
➕ Off map to north
BC Museum of Mining ✉️ Hwy 99,
Britannia Beach ☎️ 1-800/896-4044
🕐 May to mid-Oct daily 9–4.30. Closed
Sat–Sun mid-Oct to May ✋ Moderate

SUNSHINE COAST
The Sunshine Coast lies between
Vancouver and Lund, by Hwy 101
and three ferry crossings at Horseshoe
Bay, Sechelt and Egmont. A suc-
cession of beaches, mountains and
rugged headlands, dotted with small
settlements, it lacks the splendor of
much of British Columbia. Visitors
who are short of time should
plump for Bowen Island, at the
start of the coast, or Victoria or the
Gulf Islands, or take a bus along
the route.
➕ Off map to west Malaspina Coachlines
operates buses from Vancouver to Powell
River

*Escape to the Squamish Mountains
for outdoor pursuits*

*The beauty of the
wilderness at Squamish*

Historic Victoria

A walk around the Inner Harbour and the heart of the old town reveals the best of Victoria's small historic core.

DISTANCE: 2.5km (1.5 miles)   **ALLOW:** 2–3 hours

START

ROYAL BC MUSEUM (RBCM)

❶ Visit the RBCM (▷ 98, 99) and neighboring Helmcken House and St. Anne's Pioneer Schoolhouse, then walk west on Belleville Street to see the Parliament Buildings.

❷ Walk along the waterfront promenade or follow Government Street north, passing the historic Empress Hotel on the right.

❸ Victoria's visitor center is beyond the hotel on the left near the junction of Government and Humboldt streets.

❹ Follow Government Street two blocks north and turn left on Broughton Street, then right on Wharf Street. Turn right on View Street into Bastion Square, heart of the old town and home to the Maritime Museum.

END

INNER HARBOUR

❽ Turn right down Broad Street, perhaps with lunch at Pagliacci's (▷ 106), then right on Broughton and first left into Gordon Street and then right into Courtney Street for the return walk left on Government to the harbor.

❼ Cross Government Street and turn right on Broad Street, second right down pretty Trounce Alley, then left on Government Street and second left down Fort Street.

❻ Double back west on Johnson Street, turn right on Store Street then second right on Fisgard Street. Take Fan Tan Alley on the right, once full of brothels and opium dens, and turn left on Pandora Avenue.

❺ Rebar (▷ 106) is a good place for a drink or snack. Walk north from Bastion Square on Langley Street, turn left on Yates Street, then first right down the alley to Johnson Street. Explore the shops of Market Square off Johnson Street.

Entertainment and Nightlife

ENTERTAINMENT AND NIGHTLIFE

Victoria

CANOE
www.canoebrewpub.com
A converted former
power station, still with
an industrial feel (robust
walls, thick wooden
beams), provides an
impressive setting for one
of Victoria's most popular
bars. It offers own-brewed
beer, a restaurant serving
multiethnic dishes, plus
simpler pub food and
light meals from the bar.
Waterfront terrace.
➕ Off map ✉ 450 Swift
Street ☎ 250/361-1940
🕐 Sun–Fri 11am–midnight,
Sat 11am–1am

D'ARCY'S
www.darcyspub.ca
An Irish-themed pub in
the heart of the old town.
Live Irish and other music
most nights and standard
pub food. The Irish Times
(1200 Government
Street) is similar.
➕ Off map ✉ 1127 Wharf
Street ☎ 250/380-1322
🕐 Daily11am–1am

SPINNAKERS
www.spinnakers.com
Serves around 40
different beers, including
several own-brewed
ales (brewery tours
available). Occasional
live music, harbor views
and a restaurant with fine
seafood draw a mixed
and laid-back clientele.
➕ Off map ✉ 308
Catherine Street at Esquimalt
☎ 250/384-6613 🕐 Daily
11–11

Whistler

BUFFALO BILL'S
www.buffalobills.ca
A 30-something club and
bar with a modest dance
floor, DJs, comedy shows
and theme nights.
➕ Off map ✉ 4122 Village
Green ☎ 604/932-6613
🕐 Daily 8pm–2am, kitchen
closes at 10pm

DUBH LINN GATE
www.dubhlinngate.com
Irish-style pub offering a
large selection of whiskies
and beers on tap, plus
pub food and live Celtic
and other music nightly.
➕ Off map ✉ Pan Pacific,
4320 Sundial Crescent
☎ 1-800/387-3311 🕐 Daily
7am–1am

Whistler is not really the
place for theater and classical music, nor is there much
call for the performing arts
there. Victoria is a different
matter, and has numerous
festivals, including the major
JazzFest (☎ 250/388-4423;
www.jazzvictoria.ca) in June.
Visit www.victoria.ca for a
full list of festivals. The city's
main performance space for
theater and classical music
is the McPherson Playhouse
(☎ 250/386-6121 or 1-888/
717-6121; www.rmts.bc.ca).
Details of what's on can be
obtained online, from the
visitor center (▷ 99) or from
the local daily paper, the
Times-Colonist.

GARFINKEL'S
www.garfswhistler.com
Whistler's largest club,
"Garf's" offers mainstream
dance music most nights
(Thursday is the most
popular), with the occa-
sional live band. Attracts
a younger crowd than
Buffalo Bill's.
➕ Off map ✉ 4308 Mains
Street, Villa North ☎ 604/932-
2323 🕐 Daily 8pm until late

MOE JOE'S
www.moejoes.com
Smaller than Garf's but
almost as popular, and
a better place to dance.
Friday and Monday are
the busiest nights.
➕ Off map ✉ 4115 Golfer's
Approach ☎ 604/935-1152
🕐 Wed–Sat 8pm until late,
but see website for latest hours

SAVAGE BEAGLE
www.savagebeagle.ca
A long-established club
on two levels (there's a
good pub on the upper
level) that attracts a similar 30-something crowd
to Buffalo Bill's. Tuesday
is usually the big night.
➕ Off map ✉ 4222 Village
Stroll ☎ 604/938-3337
🕐 Contact for latest hours

TOMMY AFRICA'S
www.tommyafricas.com
Whistler's best-known
club has been around
since 1988. A reliable
choice for a good
night out.
➕ Off map ✉ 4216
Gateway Drive ☎ 604/932-
6090 🕐 Mon–Sat 9pm–2am,
Sun 9pm–1am

Restaurants

PRICES

Prices are approximate, based on a 3-course meal for one person.

$$$	over $40
$$	$20–$40
$	under $20

Gulf Islands

LA BERENGERIE ($–$$)

www.galiano.gulfislands.com/laberengerie

A beautiful wooden restaurant in a pleasant wooded setting 2km (1.2 miles) from Montagu Harbour, one of Galiano Island's two ferry terminals. The French owners turn local ingredients into Gallic-influenced dishes.
➕ Off map ✉ Corner of Montague and Clanton roads, Galiano Island ☎ 250/539-5392 🕐 Daily 5–11pm

HOUSE PICCOLO ($$–$$$)

www.housepiccolo.com

The place for a treat on Salt Spring, this smart restaurant in the main village has been a favorite of islanders since 1992, and has won many awards for its food and its excellent wine list, which includes several local vintages.
➕ Off map ✉ 108 Hereford Avenue, Ganges, Salt Spring Island ☎ 250/537-1844 🕐 Daily 5–11

HUMMINGBIRD PUB ($)

www.galiano.gulfislands.com/hummingbird

Galiano Island's main pub is 2km (1.2 miles) from Sturdies Bay, the second of the island's two ferry terminals (▷ left), and offers decent pub food. It also has a terrace outside.
➕ Off map ✉ 47 Sturdies Bay Road, Galiano Island ☎ 250/539-5472 🕐 Sun–Thu 11am–midnight, Fri–Sat 11am–1am

TREEHOUSE CAFÉ ($)

Pretty café and restaurant for breakfast, lunch and dinner, with varied cuisine, outdoor seating in summer, and live,

GOURMET SHOPPING

Victoria not only offers an excellent range of places to eat and drink, but also has some first-rate gourmet shops. Two of the best known are Roger's Chocolates (✉ 913 Government Street ☎ 250/727-6851; www.rogerschocolates.com) and Murchies (✉ 1110 Government Street ☎ 250/381-5451; www.murchies.com), which offers coffees, teas and other gourmet food. You'll also find many specialist food stores in and around Market Square. If you want to buy local Vancouver Island or other British Columbia wine, visit The Wine Barrel (✉ 644 Broughton Street ☎ 250/388-0606; www.thewinebarrel.com), which also sells locally produced gourmet and organic produce.

easy-listening acoustic music some nights.
➕ Off map ✉ 106 Purvis Lane, Salt Spring Island ☎ 250/537-5379 🕐 Daily 8–8 or later

Victoria

BRASSERIE L'ÉCOLE ($)

www.lecole.ca

The best French restaurant in Victoria has won numerous richly deserved awards. Menus change daily, prices are reasonable and dishes include classics such as moules, steaks and fresh fish.
➕ Off map ✉ 1715 Government Street ☎ 250/475-6260 🕐 Tue–Sat 5.30–11

DEMITASSE ($)

Relaxed but elegant café that's been popular with everyone from students to shoppers for years. Coffee, salads, sandwiches and lunchtime snacks and light meals.
➕ Off map ✉ 1320 Blanshard Street at Pandora Avenue ☎ 250/386-4442 🕐 Mon–Fri 7–4, Sat–Sun 9–2

JOHN'S PLACE ($)

www.johnsplace.ca

A perfect spot for lunch or brunch, with diner-style food, a bustling atmosphere, high ceilings, wood floors and memorabilia-lined walls.
➕ Off map ✉ 723 Pandora Avenue ☎ 250/389-0711 🕐 Mon–Thu 7am–9pm, Fri 7am–10pm, Sat 8am–10pm, Sun 8am–9pm

MO:LÉ ($)

www.molerestaurant.ca
Sleek and pared-down restaurant with bare-brick walls and wood floors that attracts a trendy crowd for brunch and classic (and occasionally adventurous) fusion and West Coast dishes. Live music on Friday and Saturday nights.
🚹 Off map ✉ 554 Pandora Avenue ☎ 250/385-6653 🕙 Daily 8–4, plus Fri–Sat 6–11pm

PAGLIACCI'S ($)

A lively Italian restaurant, with fair prices and occasional live music, that is a popular fixture of Victoria's dining scene.
🚹 Off map ✉ 1011 Broad Street at Fort ☎ 250/386-1662 🕙 Mon–Thu 11.30–10, Fri–Sat 11.30–11, Sun 10–10

REBAR ($)

www.rebarmodernfood.com
Tremendous café and juice bar, with an array of freshly made juices, smoothies and health drinks. Also offers a range of teas, coffees and organic and vegetarian snacks and light meals.
🚹 Off map ✉ 50 Bastion Square at Langley ☎ 250/361-9223 🕙 Mon–Wed 8.30am–9pm, Thu–Sat 8.30am–10pm, Sun 8.30–3.30

IL TERRAZZO ($$)

www.ilterrazzo.com
A fixture of the city for many years, the success of this restaurant is based on excellent Italian food,

a relaxed air and an attractive dining area, plus a summer patio.
🚹 Off map ✉ 555 Johnson Street, Waddington Alley ☎ 250/361-0028 🕙 Mon–Fri 11.30–3, 5–10; Sat–Sun 5–10

Whistler

APRÈS ($$$)

www.apresrestaurant.com
A cool and contemporary 50-cover dining room is the setting for elaborate and accomplished French-influenced West Coast cooking. Eat à la carte or opt for a tasting menu at around $85.
🚹 Off map ✉ 4338 Main Street ☎ 604/935-0200 🕙 Daily 6pm–midnight

ARAXI ($$$)

www.araxi.com
Among Whistler's best restaurants for many years, offering creative

TIME FOR TEA

You only need to be in Victoria for about five minutes to realise that this is a city that still plays up to its old links with Britain. Nowhere is this more clear than in the ritual of afternoon tea, a pastime you can indulge in considerable style—and expense—in the Tea Lounge of the Empress hotel. Another popular spot for tea is the Blethering Place (2250 Oak Bay Avenue), where you sip Earl Grey and nibble scones against a background of royal memorabilia.

Italian and West Coast dishes, plus a seafood bar, terrace and an extensive wine cellar.
🚹 Off map ✉ 4222 Village Square ☎ 604/932-4540 🕙 Daily 5–11

BEARFOOT BISTRO ($$$)

www.bearfootbistro.com
Once a humble bistro, now one of Canada's most celebrated restaurants, with outstanding, French food. Choose from set or tasting menus. An oyster bar offers lighter and less expensive options. Reservations essential.
🚹 Off map ✉ 4121 Village Green ☎ 604/932-3433 🕙 Call for latest hours

CITTA BISTRO ($$)

www.cittabistro.com
American-style bistro-diner offering pizzas, gourmet burgers, club sandwiches and the like. The terrace is good for people-watching, and it's a fun place for a drink later on.
🚹 Off map ✉ 4217 Village Stroll ☎ 604/932-4177 🕙 Mon–Fri 10am–1am, Sat–Sun 9am–1am

INGRID'S VILLAGE CAFÉ ($)

www.ingridswhistler.com
Loved by locals and resort workers for coffee, wraps, sandwiches, veggie burgers and soup specials.
🚹 Off map ✉ 4305 Skiers' Approach-Village Square ☎ 604/932-7000 🕙 Daily from 7.30am

Vancouver offers numerous accommodations possibilities, from luxury hotels to many hundreds of homey B&Bs. The best options are in central Downtown, close to the main sights, or in the quieter reaches of the West End.

Introduction

Base yourself on the Downtown peninsula, preferably close to its heart—the corner of Robson and Burrard streets. Alternatively, aim for one of the hotels in the West End district, less convenient for some sights, but peaceful and close to Stanley Park.

Where to stay

Downtown has most of the city's luxury hotels, usually high-rise towers with fine views. But it also has numerous budget and mid-range choices, including two hostels and an excellent YWCA. The best Downtown prices will be the same as those in the motels on the city's fringes. Avoid the district east of Gastown, and note that the southern reaches of Granville Street—though improving—are seedy in parts and badly placed for the sights. Yaletown and Granville Island have limited options.

Alternative accommodations

Vancouver has hundreds of B&Bs. While many are delightful and often beautifully located (usually in quiet areas of North or West Vancouver), they are rarely less expensive than hotels; they are also rarely in Downtown (the West End has a handful), making them inconvenient. If you're traveling with a family, or wish to save money on food, so-called "apartment'" or mid-price "suite" hotels, many of which are found on Robson Street, offer self-catering facilities and room for extra beds. Booking is highly recommended for all accommodations, especially between June and September; consult the main visitor center (▷ 122) if you arrive without a room.

Accommodations options in Vancouver are as diverse as the city itself so there is plenty of choice

VICTORIA HOTELS

Victoria's most famous luxury hotel is the Fairmont Empress (721 Government Street; www.fairmont.com). At the other extreme is the HI Hostel (516 Yates Street; www.hihostels.ca). Low-cost options include the James Bay Inn (270 Government Street; www.jamesbayinn.com). The best contemporary hotel is the Laurel Point Inn (680 Montréal Street: www.laurelpointinn.com).

Budget Hotels

PRICES

Expect to pay up to $150 per night for a double room in a budget hotel.

BOSMAN'S HOTEL

www.bosmanshotel.com
An old-style, rather dated motel, but excellent value, friendly service and a good Downtown location. Its on-site restaurant, Grill on Ninth, is popular and there's a small pool. Try to avoid noisy front-facing ground-floor rooms.
➕ M4 ✉ 1060 Howe Street at Nelson ☎ 604/682-3171 or 1-888-267-6267
Ⓖ Granville 🚌 5

BUCHAN HOTEL

www.buchanhotel.com
In a heritage building on a tree-lined street close to Stanley Park. Most rooms are modest, and have shared bathrooms, but there are also larger and better-appointed (and more expensive) options with private bathrooms. Service is cheerful.
➕ K3 ✉ 1906 Haro Street at Chilco ☎ 604/685-5354 or 1-800-668-6654 🚌 5

KINGSTON HOTEL

www.kingstonhotelvancouver.com
One of the best-known budget hotels in the city, so book ahead. Most rooms are small and dated, and not all are en-suite, but the hotel is clean, well-run and has pleasant public areas.
➕ M4 ✉ 757 Richards Street at Robson ☎ 604/684-9024 or 1-888/713-3304
Ⓖ Granville 🚌 5, 6, 8, 20

SUNSET INN & SUITES

www.sunsetinn.com
A modern high-rise "apartment" hotel on the edge of West End, and a good longer-stay option, thanks to weekly deals and self-catering facilities in most rooms.
➕ L4 ✉ 1111 Burnaby Street at Thurlow ☎ 604/688-2474 or 1-800/786-1997
🚌 5

SYLVIA HOTEL

www.sylviahotel.com
Lovely, ivy-covered 1912 landmark building with lots of old-world charm and a pretty position on English Bay Beach, near Stanley Park. The 112 rooms vary greatly in price, and the cheapest go quickly. Also apartment suites with kitchens.
➕ K3 ✉ 1154 Gifford Street ☎ 604/681-9321 🚌 5

HOSTELS

Vancouver has many hostels, from three accredited to Hosteling International, which often have hotel-like rooms and facilities, to several lively and less salubrious options. The calm HI Vancouver Downtown (1114 Burnaby Street at Thurlow; www.hihostels.ca) in the West End offers private doubles plus dorm beds (and is good for families). The Samesun (1018 Granville Street; www.samesun.com) will suit young backpackers.

VANCOUVER CENTRAL HOSTEL

www.hihostels.ca
More hotel than hostel, this is the newest and smartest of the city's official HI hostels, with private en-suite doubles or quads, most with TV and air-conditioning. Also has a kitchen, pub, laundry and other facilities.
➕ M5 ✉ 1025 Granville Street at Nelson ☎ 604/685-5335 or 1-888/203-8333
Ⓖ Burrard 🚌 5

VICTORIAN HOTEL

www.victorianhotel.ca
Two well-restored buildings from 1898. Many rooms have period features. Cheaper rooms have shared bathrooms. The best options are in the newer extension.
➕ M4 ✉ 514 Homer Street at West Pender ☎ 604/681-6369 or 1-877/681-6369
Ⓖ Granville 🚌 6, 8, 10, 20, 50, N20

YWCA HOTEL

www.ywcahotel.com
Excellent Downtown accommodations in a purpose-built building. Plain but well-equipped rooms over 11 floors, plus fitness center, laundry, cafeteria and kitchens.
➕ M5 ✉ 733 Beatty Street at West Georgia ☎ 604/895-5830 or 1-800/663-1424
Ⓖ Stadium 🚌 5

Mid-Range Hotels

PRICES

Expect to pay between $150 and $250 per night for a double room in a mid-range hotel.

BARCLAY HOTEL
www.barclayhotel.com
One of the better and most reasonably priced hotels at the northern end of Robson Street. The 90 rooms are variously priced, but remember that Robson is a busy street and noise can be an issue.
⊞ L4 ✉ 1348 Robson Street at Jervis ☎ 604/688-8850 🚌 5

BARCLAY HOUSE B&B
www.barclayhouse.com
This sophisticated and award-winning B&B offers six stylish and spacious rooms with bathrooms, plus gourmet breakfasts. It occupies a heritage building in the West End, and has a designer look, with lots of contemporary art, Wi-Fi and other thoughtful touches. The Garden Suite is a gem.
⊞ L4 ✉ 1351 Barclay Street at Jervis ☎ 604/605-1351 or 1-800/971-1351 🚌 5

BLUE HORIZON
www.bluehorizonhotel.com
A 214-room, 31-floor hotel in a converted 1960s apartment building. The spacious, air-conditioned rooms were renovated in 2000, and have a neat, contemporary look

(plus balconies), though bathrooms are rather small; higher rooms have views. There's a pleasant café with a terrace, and a decent in-house bistro (Inlets) plus the Shenanigan's lounge and nightclub.
⊞ L4 ✉ 1225 Robson Street at Bute ☎ 604/688-1411 or 1-800/633-1333 🚇 Burrard 🚌 5

CENTURY PLAZA
www.century-plaza.com
Renovated high-rise hotel with 236 standard business-traveler rooms, but a good location three blocks south of Robson Street and lots of added extras, including a first-rate spa, indoor pool, the Yuk Yuk's comedy club and a good lounge-restaurant, Figment.
⊞ L4 ✉ 1015 Burrard Street at Nelson ☎ 604/687-0575 or 1-800/663-1818 🚇 Burrard 🚌 2, 22

HOTEL LISTINGS

Browse B&Bs online at established agencies such as BB Canada (www.bbcanada.com) or the British Columbia B&B Innkeepers' Guild (www.bcsbestbnbs.com). You can book B&Bs and hotels at Vancouver's main visitor center (▷ 122) or online at www.tourismvancouver.com, or the official British Columbia site (www.hellobc.com). Sites often carry offers and last-minute or seasonal deals.

COAST PLAZA HOTEL & SUITES
www.coasthotels.com
A popular 269-room, 35-floor West End hotel, perfect for Stanley Park, the buzz of Denman Street and English Bay Beach. Not quite the value it once was, however, and the rooms are slightly showing their age. Gym and pool, plus many other facilities.
⊞ K4 ✉ 1763 Comox Street at Denman ☎ 604/688-7711 or 1-800/716-6199 🚇 Burrard 🚌 6

GRANVILLE ISLAND HOTEL
www.granvilleislandhotel.com
Modern, 85-room boutique hotel some way from most sights, but ideal for Granville Island, one of the city's most tempting attractions. Many rooms have city and waterfront views, though you pay a premium for the location. Good on-site brewpub and restaurant.
⊞ L6 ✉ 1253 Johnston Street ☎ 604/683-7373 or 1-800/663-1840 🚌 50

HOWARD JOHNSON
www.hojovancouver.com
There is nothing bland about this hotel, despite being part of a family-friendly chain. The 110 rooms over five floors are stylish—some have self-catering facilities—prices are fair, and the location is on a part of Granville Street that becomes more gentrified by the year.

🚇 L5 ✉ 1176 Granville Street at Davie ☎ 604/688-8701 or 1-888/654-6336 🚈 Burrard 🚌 4, 6, 7, 10, 50

LONSDALE QUAY HOTEL

www.lonsdalequayhotel.com
Perfect if you wish to spend a lot of time in North Vancouver. The hotel is bright and modern, and the 70 tasteful rooms (specify a waterfront view) include some designated family rooms.

🚇 d2 ✉ 123 Carrie Cates Court ☎ 604/986-6111 or 1-800/836-6111 🚈 Waterfront and then SeaBus to Lonsdale Quay

'O CANADA' HOUSE

www.ocanadahouse.com
A seven-room, antique-filled B&B in a house built in 1897 by Ewing Duchan, who wrote the Canadian national anthem here in 1909. A central but tranquil spot, with an appealing veranda and garden. Children under 12 not allowed.

🚇 L4 ✉ 1114 Barclay Street at Thurlow ☎ 604/688-0555 or 1-877/688-1114 🚌 5

RIVIERA HOTEL

www.rivieraonrobson.com
Another Robson Street hotel (formerly a 1960s apartment building), five blocks from Stanley Park. Rooms are comfortable and feature kitchenettes, making them good for longer stays and groups or families. North-facing rooms have views and prices are some of the lowest of the Robson Street hotels.

🚇 L4 ✉ 1431 Robson Street at Nicola ☎ 604/685-1301 or 1-888/699-5222 🚈 Burrard 🚌 5

ROBSONSTRASSE HOTEL & SUITES

www.robsonstrassehotel.com
One of the best of several multistory hotels on Robson Street offers a variety of rooms and self-catering suites at a range of prices. Rooms are air-conditioned and parking is available.

🚇 L4 ✉ 1394 Robson Street at Broughton ☎ 604/687-1674 or 1-888/667-0877 🚈 Burrard 🚌 5

ROSEDALE ON ROBSON

www.rosedaleonrobson.com
Large, high-rise, 1990s hotel near the public library. Caters well for families, offering one- and two-bedroom suites, with kitchenettes, plus designated family rooms. Rooms are comfortable, if unexceptional (those on the top floors are best), but the indoor pool is excellent. Popular with tour groups.

🚇 M5 ✉ 838 Hamilton Street at Robson ☎ 604/689-8033 or 1-800/661-8870 🚈 Burrard 🚌 5

SANDMAN HOTEL DOWNTOWN

www.sandman.ca
On the dowdier eastern fringe of Downtown, the Sandman is part of a reliable chain with hotels in many Canadian cities. Rooms are comfortable, if bland, but there are plenty of added extras, such as pool, fitness center and a lively sports bar and restaurant.

🚇 M4 ✉ 180 West Georgia Street at Homer ☎ 604/681-2211 or 1-800/726-3626 🚈 Granville 🚌 5

WEST END GUESTHOUSE

www.westendguesthouse.com
Eight elegant rooms in an upscale B&B in a 1906 town house. Lots of antiques and period details, with sherry and iced tea in the afternoon, plus many touches you'd normally only expect in a smart hotel.

🚇 L4 ✉ 1362 Haro Street at Jervis ☎ 604/681-2889 or 1-888/546-3327 🚌 5

WHISTLER HOTELS

To enjoy Whistler's recreational opportunities properly, you'll need to spend a night in the resort. In winter, most rooms are sold as part of ski packages. In summer, things are more flexible, but be sure to book. Use the accommodations service www.whistlerblackcomb.com or try the central and well-priced Blackcomb Lodge (www.blackcomblodge.com) or small Chalet Luise B&B (www.chaletluise.com).

Luxury Hotels

PRICES

Expect to pay more than $250 per night for a double room in a luxury hotel.

FAIRMONT HOTEL VANCOUVER

www.fairmont.com
The *grande dame* of Vancouver hotels; the château-style exterior is a city landmark. Rooms are traditionally decorated and fitted and the bars and restaurants are also good for nonpatrons. First choice for prestigious, old-world comfort.
✚ M4 ✉ 900 West Georgia Street at Burrard ☎ 604/684-3131 or 1-800/257-7544 🚇 Burrard 🚌 2, 5, 22, 32 and all city center services

FAIRMONT WATERFRONT

www.fairmont.com
More modern (1991) than its sister hotel, the Hotel Vancouver, and with tasteful but less striking rooms and public spaces. The position near Canada Place is excellent; top floors have views.
✚ M4 ✉ 900 Canada Place Way ☎ 604/691-1991 or 1-800/441-1414 🚇 Waterfront or Burrard 🚌 6, 50 and all city center services

FOUR SEASONS VANCOUVER

www.fourseason.com
A central 28-floor hotel with Four Seasons' trademark service. Rooms and public spaces are superb:

Try the Garden Terrace for a breakfast treat, even if you are not staying.
✚ M4 ✉ 791 West Georgia Street at Howe ☎ 604/689-9333 or 1-800/819-5053 🚇 Burrard 🚌 5, 50 and all city center services

LODEN HOTEL

www.lodenvancouver.com
Vancouver's latest luxury hotel is an intimate temple to modern design. Its 77 rooms have state-of-the-art technology and facilities. It is close to Coal Harbour, and much is expected of its signature restaurant, Voya.
✚ M4 ✉ 1177 Melville Street at Bute ☎ 604/669-5060 or 1-877/225-6336 🚌 5

OPUS HOTEL

www.opushotel.com
Hip 96-room boutique hotel in Yaletown, so not ideal for sightseeing, but first choice in the city if you want a hotel that is trendy without pretension. Rooms have five different

CUTTING COSTS

Hotel websites often have offers that can bring reductions of up to 50 percent. Also, most hotels will put a third bed in a room for a few dollars. Some hotels allow children under a certain age—typically 12—to stay free if they share their parents' room. Prices often exclude taxes of up to 16 percent, though foreign visitors can reclaim some of these.

decorative schemes, from minimalist to eclectic.
✚ M5 ✉ 322 Davie Street at Hamilton ☎ 604/642-6787 or 1-866/642-6787 🚇 Yaletown-Roundhouse 🚌 6, 15, C23, N23

PAN PACIFIC

www.panpacific.com
This high-rise convention hotel at the heart of Canada Place has a stunning lobby. Its rooms can also be small, though the views are spectacular.
✚ M4 ✉ 999 Canada Place Way ☎ 604/662-8111 or 1-800/663-1515 🚇 Waterfront or Burrard 🚌 6, 50 and all city center services

SUTTON PLACE HOTEL

www.suttonplace.com
This hotel opened in 1986 and is top-rated among the city's luxury hotels. Despite a bland exterior it is popular with celebrities. All rooms have the latest high-tech facilities.
✚ M4 ✉ 845 Burrard Street at Robson ☎ 604/682-5511 or 1-866/378-8866 🚇 Burrard 🚌 5

WEDGEWOOD HOTEL

www.wedgewoodhotel.com
This privately owned, 83-room hotel, with the Opus and Loden, is among the most intimate of Vancouver's luxury hotels. Rooms are opulent and spacious (but avoid rear-facing rooms).
✚ M4 ✉ 845 Hornby Street at Robson ☎ 604/689-7777 or 1-800/663-0666 🚇 Burrard 🚌 5

This section contains essential information about preparing for your journey to Vancouver, how to get around once you are there, and other practicalities.

Need to Know

Planning Ahead

When to Go

The best time to visit Vancouver is between June and August. Although the city has a reputation for rain, only 10 percent of the year's total falls in June, July and August. The good weather often extends into September and October, when the city will also be less crowded.

TIME

L Vancouver is eight hours behind GMT and three hours behind New York. Clocks go forward one hour for summer time.

AVERAGE DAILY MAXIMUM TEMPERATURES

JAN	FEB	MAR	APR	MAY	JUN	JUL	AUG	SEP	OCT	NOV	DEC
41°F	44°F	50°F	57°F	64°F	69°F	73°F	73°F	64°F	57°F	48°F	43°F
5°C	7°C	10°C	14°C	18°C	21°C	23°C	23°C	18°C	14°C	9°C	6°C

Spring (May–June) is generally mild, with a mixture of wet and sunny days. On average, May has ten rainy days, June six.

Summer (July–August) can be hot, with clear skies and little rain. July has an average of six rainy days, August eight.

Autumn (September–October) is often still warm or mild. September has an average of nine rainy days, October 16.

Winter (November–April) is mild and damp, but with no snow. December and January have 20 rainy days each, November 18, February and March 15.

WHAT'S ON

January *Chinese New Year*: 15 days of festivities in Chinatown and elsewhere.

February *Boat Show*: Western Canada's largest and oldest boat show is held in the BC Stadium over five days at the start of the month.

May *Vancouver Marathon* (first Sun): Canada's largest marathon attracts more than 6,000 runners (www. bmovancouvermarathon.ca).

Children's Festival (end May–early Jun): a week's events in Vanier Park attract 70,000 people (www. childrensfestival.ca).

June *Bard on the Beach* (Jun–Sep): Shakespeare plays performed outdoors

(www.bardonthebeach.org).

Jazz Festival: (10 days at end of month): some 800 jazz and blues musicians perform at 25 venues around the city (www.coastaljazz.ca).

July *Folk Festival* (3rd weekend): 30,000 people and 100 performers come to Jericho Beach Park.

Celebration of Light: world's largest firework competition attracts 500,000 people to English Bay over four nights.

August *Abbotsford Air Show*: excellent air shows 58km (36 miles) from the city (www. abbotsfordairshow.com).

Pride Parade: colorful parade and events celebrating Vancouver's gay and

lesbian community (www. vancouverpride.ca).

September *Fringe Theatre Festival*: theater, comedy and dance groups perform more than 500 shows.

Film Festival: North America's third-largest film festival; more than 500 screenings (www.viff.org).

November *VanDusen Market and Festival of Light* (late Nov–Dec): gift and craft market in the VanDusen Botanical Garden, illuminated with 20,000 lights.

December *Christmas Carol Ship Parade* (three weeks to Christmas): magical flotillas of illuminated boats with carol singers in the harbor.

Useful Websites

www.city.vancouver.bc.ca
Vancouver's official civic site, with lots of information and links, plus downloadable city maps.

www.discovervancouver.com
A comprehensive commercial site offering detailed information on where to eat and stay, events, festivals and city attractions.

www.hellobc.com
Official tourism site for British Columbia. Plenty of information on Vancouver and Victoria, plus help with booking accommodations.

www.tourismvancouver.com
Vancouver's official visitor information site is packed with information for planning your trip and enjoying your stay in the city.

www.urbandiner.ca
Visit this site for the latest on new restaurants and cafés, plus tips on dining out in the city.

www.straight.com
The online version of *Georgia Straight*, Vancouver's leading listings magazine, with reviews, features, events, and full entertainment and other listings.

www.ticketmaster.ca
Online ticket booking service for numerous shows and events around the city. Also visit www.ticketstonight.ca for last-minute and discounted same-day tickets.

www.vancouver2010.com
The official site for the 2010 Vancouver Winter Olympics.

www.visitorschoice.com
Comprehensive commercial site with details of dining, festivals, accommodations, attractions and more.

GOOD TRAVEL SITES

www.fodors.com
A complete travel-planning site. Research prices and the weather; reserve air tickets, cars and rooms; ask questions (and get answers) from fellow visitors; and find links to other sites.

www.bcferries.com
BC Ferries runs ferry services to Vancouver Island and the Gulf Islands from two terminals north and south of the city center.

CYBERCAFÉS

Visit http://vancouver.wifimug.org for a current list of the many cafés around the city that offer free Wi-Fi.

Internet Coffee
🔲 L4 ✉ 1104 Davie Street at Thurlow ☎ 604/682-6668 🕐 9am late 💷 $2 an hour

Star Internet
🔲 L3 ✉ 1690 Robson Street at Bidwell ☎ 604/685-645 🕐 Daily 24 hours 💷 $2 an hour

Vancouver Public Library
🔲 M5 ✉ 350 West Georgia Street at Robson and Homer ☎ 604/331-3603 🕐 Mon–Thu 10–9, Fri–Sat 10–6, Sun 12–5 💷 Free Wi-Fi

NEED TO KNOW PLANNING AHEAD

Getting There

ENTRY REQUIREMENTS

Most visitors to Canada need a valid passport, though at the time of writing US travelers entering Canada could use other proof of citizenship and identity. All US travelers returning to the United States by air, however, must have a passport; this requirement is due to be extended to re-entry by land or sea in June 2009. See www.travel.state.gov (or www.dhs.gov) for the latest information on documents, including passport cards. Check with your Canadian embassy or consulate or visit the Citizen & Immigration Canada website (www.cic.gc.ca) for this and other visa requirements. Although visas are not currently required for UK, US, Australian, New Zealand, Irish or EU nationals (provided the stay is no longer than three months), it is best to check before you travel.

INSURANCE

Check your policy and buy any necessary supplements. It is vital that travel insurance covers medical expenses, in addition to accidents, trip cancellation, baggage loss and theft. Check the policy covers any treatment for a chronic condition. The European Health Insurance Card available to EU nationals is not valid in Canada.

AIRPORT

Most national and all international airlines fly to Vancouver International Airport, 10km (6 miles) south of Downtown. International flights arrive at a majestic new terminal and national flights at the smaller and linked old main terminal.

30km (18 miles)
20km (12 miles)
10km (6 miles)

✈ Vancouver International Airport

FROM THE AIRPORT

Vancouver International Airport (☎ 604/207-7077; www.yvr.ca) is modern and efficient, with international and national terminals, plus the small South Terminal on the Fraser River for seaplanes and other small aircraft: The last is linked to the main airport by free shuttle buses. Other intercity seaplanes from Victoria land near Canada Place (▷ 119).

The best way from the airport to Downtown is on SkyTrain (☎ 604/953-3333; www.translink.ca), the city's light-transit system (▷ 118–119). From November 2009, SkyTrain's new Canada Line (www.canadaline.ca) runs from the airport to Waterfront Station near Canada Place in Downtown. Alternatively, take the Airporter shuttle bus (☎ 604/946-8866 or 1-800/668-3141; www.yvrairporter.com), which leaves from outside the International Arrivals terminal every 20 to 30 minutes (5.20am to 11.45pm). Journey time is 35–45 minutes, depending on traffic. The bus runs a variety of routes (friendly staff help you choose the best route) and has the advantage of calling at around 25 major Downtown and

other hotels. The cost is $13.75 one-way, $21.50 round-trip (return). Purchase tickets at the departure point. Taxis to Downtown cost $30–$35; journey time is about 35 minutes.

ARRIVING BY CAR

Getting to Vancouver by car from the US or the rest of Canada is straightforward. If you are coming from eastern Canada or central US, the main Trans-Canada Highway (Hwy 1) cuts through the suburbs of southeast Vancouver before an exit at Cassiar Street to Hastings Street (Hwy 7a), which leads west 7km (4 miles) to Downtown. From the western US, take Interstate 5 (I-5) from Seattle and Washington State to the border crossing (open 24 hours) at Blaine (in the US) and White Rock (in British Columbia), 210km (130 miles) from Seattle. Interstate 5 becomes Canadian Hwy 99, and then Oak Street. At Oak Street and 70th Avenue, follow signs for Granville Street, a major artery into central Downtown.

ARRIVING BY BUS

Greyhound (☎ 1-800/661-8747; www. greyhound.ca) buses from eastern Canada and services from Victoria, Whistler and the Sunshine Coast, plus Quick Coach Lines (☎ 1-800/665-2122; www.quickcoach.com) from Seattle, arrive at Vancouver's main bus terminal (✉ 1150 Station Street), in a dismal part of the city alongside the VIA Rail Pacific Central Station. Take a taxi to Downtown ($7–$10) or the SkyTrain light transit service to Waterfront Station from Science World-Main Street station, 150m (165 yards) from the terminal.

ARRIVING BY TRAIN

Canadian VIA Rail (☎ 1-888/842-7245; www. viarail.com) services from Kamloops, Jasper and other points in eastern Canada, plus Amtrak (☎ 1-800/872-7245; www.amtrak.com) services from Eugene, Portland and Seattle, arrive at the Pacific Central Station alongside the bus terminal (▷ above).

VICTORIA AND WHISTLER

If you are arriving at Vancouver International Airport and wish to head straight to Victoria or Whistler, two bus companies offer direct services to both destinations from the airport. Pacific Coach Lines (☎ 604/662-7575 or 1-800/661-1725; www. pacificcoach.com) runs up to seven daily services to Victoria's bus terminal, inclusive of ferry crossing. Perimeter (☎ 604/266-5386 or 1-877/317-7788; www. perimeterbus.com) has up to nine daily departures to Whistler.

LOST PROPERTY

If you lose anything at the airport, contact the Customer Service Counter (☎ 604/ 276-6104 ◎ Daily 9–5.30), located on Level 3 of the International Departures Terminal. For losses on the transit system (buses, SkyTrain and SeaBus), contact Translink (☎ 604/ 682-7887). The lost property office is at the Stadium SkyTrain station (✉ 590 Beatty Street ◎ Daily 8.30–5.30). For losses in taxis (▷ 119), contact the taxi company directly.

Getting Around

MINI-FERRIES

Aquabus (☎ 604/689-5858; www.theaquabus.com) and False Creek Ferries (☎ 604/684-7781; www.granvilleislandferries.bc.ca) operate tiny boats over similar routes on False Creek, the arm of water that runs between Downtown and South Vancouver. They provide both a fun sightseeing trip and an efficient way of traveling between Granville Island (▷ 65) and Vanier Park (for the Vancouver Museum, Maritime Museum and H.R. MacMillan Space Centre), and between these and other destinations to quays in Downtown (the foot of Hornby Street), near Yaletown and at Science World (▷ 48). Tickets are inexpensive ($2.50–$5, depending on the route and distance traveled) and run daily from around 7am to 10.30pm (8.30pm in winter). Day passes cost $12 ($8 for children).

PUBLIC TRANSPORTATION

● Translink (☎ 604/953-3333; www.translink.bc.ca) is responsible for Vancouver's integrated public transportation (or transit) system, which comprises buses, the SeaBus ferry to North Vancouver, and SkyTrain, a light-rail network.

TICKETS

● Tickets are valid across all three services of the transit system for 90 minutes from the moment they are first validated. There are three zones: the Yellow Zone (Zone 1), Red (Zone 2) and Green (Zone 3), with tickets becoming more expensive in zones 2 and 3. Zone 1 covers most of Downtown, but note that the SeaBus crossing is a two-zone journey.

● Zone 1 tickets cost $2.50. Zone 2 costs $3.75, Zone 3 $5. Concessionary fares are available for seniors and children aged 3 to 13. Under-3s travel free. You may need to provide proof of your child's age. An all-zone day pass is available for $9.

● Note at weekends and public holidays, and after 6.30pm Monday to Friday, all journeys are rated as Zone 1.

● You can buy tickets at SeaBus and SkyTrain terminals or from the many stores and news-stands that carry the Translink "FareDealer" logo. Tickets can be bought on buses, but you must have the exact money: no change is given.

BUSES

● Buses cover most of the Downtown core, with bus 5 the key service on Robson Street, the city center's main east to west artery, and 50 the main service on Granville, the key north to south route. Night-bus services operate on key routes from designated stops roughly every 30 minutes from 1.30am to 3 or 4am.

SKYTRAIN

SkyTrain is an excellent three-line light-rail system (services every 4–8 minutes, Mon–Fri 5am–1am, Sat 6am–1am, Sun 7am–midnight), though its coverage does not provide a

stand-alone means of transportation around the whole city. The main line runs from Waterfront Station to the southern suburbs, with useful stops for visitors at Granville, Stadium and Science World-Main Street. The new Canada Line (due to open November 2009) runs from Waterfront Station to Vancouver International Airport (plus a branch to Richmond), with useful stops in Yaletown and close to Queen Elizabeth Park in South Vancouver.

CAR RENTAL

● You will not need a car in Vancouver or Victoria, but if you require a vehicle to travel beyond the city, then rental is straightforward. All the major car-rental companies have offices at the airport and across the city. As parking is difficult, or expensive in Downtown Vancouver, it makes sense to rent a car at the end of your stay, just before leaving the city. You must be over 21 to rent a car (sometimes over 25).
● Alamo ☎ 1-800/462-5266; www.alamo.ca
● Budget ☎ 1-800/268-8900; www.budgetbc.com
● Hertz ☎ 1-800/263-0600; www.hertz.com
● Thrifty ☎ 604/681-4389; www.thrifty.com

SEABUS

SeaBus is the 400-seat catamaran ferry (services every 15–30 minutes Mon–Sat 6.15am–12.45am, Sun 8.15am–11.15pm; journey time 12 minutes) that operates between a terminal at Waterfront Station (▷ 52) and Lonsdale Quay (▷ 88) on the North Shore in North Vancouver. At Lonsdale Quay, there is a bus terminal for services across North Vancouver, including Grouse Mountain (▷ 84).

TAXICABS

Vancouver cabs are inexpensive (from $2.70, plus $1.58 per kilometer). Cab companies include: Black Top & Checker (☎ 604/731-1111); Maclure's (☎ 604/683-6666); Vancouver Taxi (☎ 604/871-1111) and Yellow (☎ 604/681-1111). A 10 percent tip is normal.

SEAPLANES

You won't have been in Vancouver long before you see or hear the buzz of seaplanes. Some are sightseeing tours, but most are scheduled services, usually to Victoria's Inner Harbour, the Gulf Islands or farther afield. Seaplanes offer the quickest route to Victoria (35 minutes, against 3 hours 35 minutes by combined bus-ferry crossing). They also offer wonderful views of the mountains, Vancouver and the Gulf Islands en route. Two companies run similar planes, schedules and services at similar prices, both from a terminal accessed from the waterfront west of Canada Place: Harbour Air (☎ 604/274-1277 or 1-800/665-0212; www.harbour-air.com) and West Coast Air (☎ 604/606 6888 or 1-800/347-2222; www.westcoastair.com). Prices to Victoria are $130 one-way and 20-minute sightseeing tours are from $99.

Essential Facts

CURRENCY

A Canadian dollar is made up of 100 cents. The one-cent piece, or penny, is copper in color. There are also five-cent pieces (nickels), ten cent (dimes) and 25 cent (quarters). The gold-colored one-dollar piece is known as a "loonie" after the bird (a loon) on one face. The two-dollar piece, or "toonie", is silver and gold. Bills (notes) come in denominations of $5 (blue), $10 (purple), $20 (green), $50 (pink) and $100 (brown). There have been counterfeit problems with $50 and $100 notes. New designs for $5, $10 and $20 notes were recently intro-duced, but the old designs remain legal tender.

10 Canadian dollars

20 Canadian dollars

50 Canadian dollars

100 Canadian dollars

CONSULATES

● Australia:
✉ Suite 1225, 888 Dunsmuir Street at Hornby
☎ 604/684-1177
● France:
✉ 1130 West Pender Street at Thurlow
☎ 604/681-4345
● Germany:
✉ Suite 704, World Trade Centre, 999 Canada Place at Hornby
☎ 604/684-8377
● New Zealand:
✉ Suite 1200, 888 Dunsmuir Street at Hornby
☎ 604/684-7388
● Republic of Ireland:
✉ Suite 1000, 10th Floor, 100 West Pender Street at Abbott
☎ 604/683-9233
● United Kingdom:
✉ Suite 800, 1111 Melville Street at Thurlow
☎ 604/683-4421
United States:
✉ 1075 West Pender Street at Thurlow
☎ 604/685-4311

CUSTOMS REGULATIONS

● Contact the Canada Customs and Revenue Agency (☎ 204/983-3500 or 1-800/461-9999; www.ccra-adrc.gc.ca/visitors) for information.

ELECTRICITY

● Canada operates on 110V, 60-cycle electric power, like the US.
● Plugs are either two-pin (flat) or three-pin (two flat, one round). European visitors will need an adaptor.

MEDICAL AND DENTAL TREATMENT

● Medical treatment is expensive in Canada, and there are no reciprocal healthcare arrange-ments with other countries. It is essential that you have travel insurance that covers any medi-cal treatment you may need while in Canada.
● Doctors: central walk-in medical centers include the Stein Medical Clinic ✉ Bentall

5 Lobby, 550 Burrard Street at West Pender
☎ 604/688-5924; www.steinmedical.com
🕐 Mon–Fri 8.30–5.30
● Dentists: drop-in dentist at Dentacare
✉ Bentall Centre, 1055 Dunsmuir Street at
Burrard ☎ 604/669-6700 🕐 Mon–Fri 8–5. Or
contact the BC Dental Association for referrals
☎ 604/736-7202; www.bcdental.org
● Hospitals: Vancouver General ✉ 855 West
12th Avenue at Oak Street ☎ 604/875-4111;
St Paul's ✉ 1081 Burrard Street at Helmcken
☎ 604/682-2344; BC Children's Hospital
✉ 4480 Oak Street ☎ 604/875-2345
● Pharmacies: Vancouver has many
pharmacies. Shoppers Drug Mart is open
24 hours ✉ 1125 Davie Street at Thurlow
☎ 604/669-2424

NEWSPAPERS, MAGAZINES, RADIO AND TELEVISION

● Local papers include the *Vancouver Sun* and
The Province, a tabloid. *The Globe and Mail* is
the main national newspaper. US newspapers
should be available from kiosks and stores such
as Chapters (▷ 34), on the same day, but UK
and European titles can be up to a week old.
● The *Georgia Straight* (▷ 115) and other listings magazines are available free from "dump
bins" in stores and elsewhere around the city.
● The Canadian Broadcasting Corporation
(CBC) is the national TV and radio broadcaster.
● Most hotels and private homes have
cable TV, offering a plethora of local TV and
radio stations, but also a great number of
US channels.

VISITORS WITH DISABILITIES

Vancouver is an excellent city
for those with disabilities.
Designated taxis and rental
cars are available on request
and the Airporter shuttle
(▷ 116) is wheelchair-
adapted, as are SeaBus,
SkyTrain, BC Ferries and
most transit buses. Book 48
hours ahead for accessible
services aboard Greyhound
buses and Pacific Coach
Lines services to Victoria.
Virtually all major sights and
attractions have first-rate
provision for those with
disabilities. For transit
information contact Translink
(▷ 118) or visit www.
accesstotravel.gc.ca.
For further general
information visit www.
bcpara.org or www.sath.org.
Information for the visually
impaired can be found at
www.cnib.ca.

POST

● Main post office:
✉ 349 West Georgia Street
at Homer ☎ 604/662-5723;
www.canadapost.ca
🕐 Mon–Fri 8–5.30
● Post office outlets (look for
blue-and-red window signs)
with longer hours can be
found in many convenience
stores, such as 7-Eleven and
Shoppers Drug Mart.

VISITOR INFORMATION

Vancouver's main visitor center is known as the TouristInfo Centre and is located at the foot of Burrard Street just opposite the entrance to Canada Place (▷ 24–25). It provides excellent free city maps and offers a wealth of information on attractions, dining, tours, transit, shows and much more. Staff will also help with booking tours and finding accommodations. There is an ATM currency exchange plus a Tickets Tonight kiosk for same-day discount tickets to shows and concerts. There are also smaller Tourism Vancouver kiosks around the city and offices at the domestic and international terminals at Vancouver International Airport.

✉ TouristInfo Centre, 200 Burrard Street ☎ 604/683-2000; www.tourism vancouver.com ⏰ Jun–end Aug daily 8.30–6; Sep–end May Mon–Sat 8.30–5 🚇 Burrard or Waterfront 🚌 6, 44, 50

OPENING HOURS

● Banks: Most banks open Mon–Fri 9 or 9.30–5, though some may open from 8–8, plus shorter hours on Sat, but close Mon.
● Museums and attractions: Vary considerably. Many have shorter hours from Labour Day (the first Mon in Sep) to Victoria Day (third Mon in May).
● Post offices: Generally Mon–Fri 9.30–5, sometimes Sat 10–4 or similar, but outlets in convenience stores have longer hours.
● Shops: Vary considerably. Most city shops, especially those in busy or tourist areas, open daily in summer 10–8 or later; otherwise Mon–Sat 10–5. Convenience stores have longer hours, often 24 hours daily.

PUBLIC HOLIDAYS

● New Year's Day (Jan 1)
● Good Friday and Easter Monday
● Victoria Day (third Mon in May)
● Canada Day (Jul 1)
● BC Day (first Mon in Aug)
● Labour Day (first Mon in Sep)
● Thanksgiving (second Mon in Oct)
● Remembrance Day (Nov 11)
● Christmas Day (Dec 25)
● Boxing Day (Dec 26)
● Banks, schools and government offices all close on public holidays and many attractions and transportation services follow Sunday openings and timetables.
● Holidays falling on a weekend are usually taken on the following Monday.

TELEPHONES

● Outgoing: To call abroad the prefix is 011 then the country code: For the UK dial 011 44 then the number minus the "0" at the start of the code. For Australia the country code is 61, New Zealand 64 and the Republic of Ireland 353.

● Calls to the US: The exception is calls to the US, which shares the 001 international prefix with Canada. Dial 1 followed by the state or city code, then the telephone number.

● Incoming: To call Vancouver from the UK and the rest of Europe, dial 001 and then the number, including the 604 prefix.

● Calls in Vancouver: The 604 prefix must always be dialed, even when calling 604 numbers within Vancouver itself. Victoria's equivalent code is 250.

● Calls from hotels. Remember that you often pay a high tariff to use direct-dial services from hotel rooms. However, many hotels offer free local calls (604 numbers within the city).

● Mobile (cell) phones: Contact your service provider to check whether your handset will work on Canada's 1900 megaHertz network.

● Pay phones: Use ¢25 coins. Dial "0" to talk to an operator, "00" for the international operator. For directory enquiries call 411; the cost is ¢75.

TIPPING

● Tipping in Canada is widespread—more so than in the UK and the rest of Europe. Unless a charge for service is levied, tip 12–20 percent, depending on the type and quality of service.

MAPS

If you would like to supplement the maps in this guide, then the visitor center (▷ 122) provides free regularly updated maps of the main Downtown area in a convenient format. If you require more detail, the Vancouver Streetwise Map Book ($5.95) is widely available at bookshops and convenience stores. You can also download maps from the official City of Vancouver website (www.vancouver.ca/vanmap)

Timeline

GOLD FEVER

The discovery of gold in the wild interior mountains of what would later be known as British Columbia transformed the region in 1858. Some 30,000 hopefuls poured first into Victoria, then the only local staging post for supplies, before sailing across the Georgia Strait to begin their journey up the Fraser River into the interior. A garrison, New Westminster, was built to keep order, and Britain declared the interior Crown land for the first time, fearful of American ambitions in the region. The need for an ice-free harbor for New Westminster led to trails being cut the short distance north to Burrard Inlet, future site of Vancouver. By 1866, the interior and Vancouver Island Crown colonies were merged as British Columbia, which in 1871 joined the Confederation of Canada.

Simon Fraser, Chief of The Clan Fraser (left); "Gassy" Jack statue (middle); the first trans-continental train arriving in Vancouver (right)

16,000–11,000 BC First aboriginal peoples settle in the region after crossing from Asia, attracted by rich seas and forests.

1778 British seafarer Sir James Cook makes first recorded landfall in the region at Nootka Sound on Vancouver Island.

1791 Spaniard José María Narváez sails into what will be known as Burrard Inlet.

1792 Captain George Vancouver of the British Royal Navy sails into Burrard Inlet and claims the area for Britain, but leaves after 24 hours.

1808 Explorer Simon Fraser travels down Fraser River, but misses Burrard Inlet, Vancouver's future site.

1827 Hudson's Bay Company (HBC) establishes the first European settlement in BC at Fort Langley, 48km (30 miles) from the sea.

1842 HBC establishes Fort Camouson on Vancouver Island, later to change its name to Fort Victoria and then Victoria.

1846 Oregon Treaty establishes 49th parallel as border between US and British territory.

1858 Gold rushes lead to the creation of New Westminster fort on the Fraser River to control the flood of prospectors (▷ panel).

1859 Trails cut from New Westminster to Burrard Inlet. Coal discovered near present-day Stanley Park.

1867 A sawmill is built on Burrard Inlet. "Gassy" Jack Deighton's bars for the lumbermen grow into a shantytown, Gassy's Town.

1869 Gassy's Town becomes Granville, then Vancouver, but is destroyed by fire in 1886.

1887 First trans-continental train pulls into the rebuilt town.

1900 Vancouver surpasses the population of Victoria. Aboriginal settlements are displaced from Vanier Park.

1938 The Lions Gate Bridge is completed.

1956 Old wooden buildings in West End razed; marks start of high-rise building boom.

1979 Project to regenerate Granville Island.

1986 The world trade fair, Expo'86, raises Vancouver's international profile.

1995 Majestic public library opens.

2003 Vancouver is awarded the 2010 Winter Olympic Games.

2009 The rapid transit train line, Canada Line, is scheduled for completion in late 2009.

UNITED BY RAIL

In the 19th century, as more of Canada was opened up, politicians realized that something was needed to unite the country and make it more than a mere "geographical expression." The answer was the trans-continental railway, which would bind the country with steel rails and unlock the vast raw materials and agricultural riches of the Prairies and western interior. The 4,000km (2,485-mile) line was a vast engineering challenge, not least because the rails had to cross the mighty barrier of the Rockies. After decades of political intrigue, false starts and near-bankruptcy, the Canadian Pacific Railway reached the west coast in 1885, transforming the fortunes of its terminus, the little town of Granville, soon to be renamed Vancouver.

Lions Gate Suspension Bridge (left); Vancouver Public Library (right)

Index